THE TRUTH
ABOUT THINGS
THAT SUCK

THE TRUTH

ABOUT THINGS

THAT SUCK

MINDY HENDERSON

Woodhall Press
Norwalk, CT

woodhall press

Woodhall Press, 81 Old Saugatuck Road, Norwalk, CT 06855
WoodhallPress.com

Cover design: Jessica Dionne Wright
Layout artist: Amie McCracken

Library of Congress Cataloging-in-Publication Data available

ISBN 978-1-954907-07-2(paper: alk paper)
ISBN 978-1-954907-08-9(electronic)

First Edition
Distributed by Independent Publishers Group
(800) 888-4741

Printed in the United States of America

For mom and dad.
My original source of hope, strength, humor and ambition.

Table of Contents

Introduction:
The Struggle is Real

I used to think that because I was in a wheelchair, my quota of bad luck or challenges and struggles had been met. I thought I couldn't get cancer, lose a job, break a bone, have an accident, or have my heart broken. I actually remember thinking those thoughts—no kidding. I was four-ish, I think, was in my bedroom, and I remember hearing someone else was sick. And I thought to myself, "I could never get (whatever the thing was)—I'm in a wheelchair. Nothing else bad can happen." Ah, the innocence of youth, right? While it was a precious theory, it turned out to be one of the *few* times in my life when I was wrong (for real—ask my husband. I'm, like, *never* wrong.). Turns out, there actually were (and still could be...oy...) plenty of things that could go wrong, hurt me, devastate me, or could traumatize me and show up on any old Tuesday merely to be a pain in the ass.

My disability is what I would label as my "primary" adversity—my #1 challenge, struggle, and pain-in-the-ass Tuesday. I was diagnosed with a neuromuscular condition called Spinal Muscular Atrophy (SMA) when I was only about 15 months old. This is a condition that (in my incredibly simple, unscientific brain's way of explaining) affects my motor neurons' ability to function and to send messages to the muscles telling them what to do. Because of the lack of communication to the muscles, they atrophy over time. Just about every muscle in my body is affected. It's a progressive condition, which means, the sucker gets worse over time. As it gets worse, I've had to grieve the loss of the function I used to have—to be able to reach up to do my own hair, my makeup, to lift a glass up off a table, and drink from it without a straw. The list goes on. I have had corrective surgery for severe scoliosis from my weakened back and trunk muscles, but I still sit a little crooked. There is the potential for pulmonary and respiratory complications, and as a result, my lung capacity is diminished, so things like flu or COVID could be quite serious for me.

There *is* a bit of a silver lining to my condition—there are varying degrees of severity and no one case is quite like another. For you brainiacs in the crowd, it boils down to the number of copies of the SMN2 gene you have. I have three copies of it, and the more copies you have, the better off you are. Before you ask, yes, I've definitely thanked my parents for all the SMN2. It has served me well, and I've always been on the healthier end of the SMA spectrum.

When I was born, all was well—I was a normal, healthy, happy baby girl. I hit all of the major milestones babies hit—rolling, crawling, standing, walking, and talking. But then, I stopped walking and standing (continued talking like a maniac—in fact, I don't mean to brag, but my first word was a sentence. My dad came in to get me up from a nap and I looked up and said, "Hi daddy." I know, genius, right…?).

As for walking, I'm told it was almost as if I'd lost interest and couldn't be bothered to stand or walk anymore, and there were a few other signs indicating something might be wrong, so my mom took me to the pediatrician, who said I was fine and that it was likely a phase I was going through, and to let it play out.

My parents knew better. Parents know when something is wrong with their children, and their instincts were kicking in. My dad was working in a hospital and was able to get someone else to see us, and that was the first stop on the scavenger hunt it took to get my diagnosis.

Ultimately, I was diagnosed by the head of neurology at the Mayo Clinic in Minnesota. This was 1975 (ugh, okay, I'm taking one for the team and giving you the tools to calculate my age!) and there was far less known about my condition back then. As a result, my parents (who by the way, were only in their twenties when this happened and they found themselves with a sick child, having to navigate a complicated medical system to get answers) were told some really scary things—I would lose my cognitive function. I would not live to be three. While there was no cure and no treatments to speak of, the diagnosing doctor DID agree with my parents who speculated that maybe physical therapy could help. So, they tried. They wanted to know that if I were to leave this world earlier than they'd expected, that they had done everything humanly possible to help me.

I started to get stronger—it was slow, and subtle, but the improvements were irrefutable. And then I had a third birthday, and a fourth. And many more after that. AND, I am sitting here writing these words—cognition fully intact. (Although, most mornings that little miracle requires a lot of coffee...) The sentence of life in a wheelchair was real, however, no probation, no parole, no early-release for good behavior (and I've tried SO hard to be good, y'all!). So, life in a wheelchair, it shall be.

Here is the thing, though. This story is not one I remember living, of course—it's one of those stories that you just always know your entire life. I don't remember who told it to me first, but I've always had the knowledge of how this all went down. And because of that, my parents became my first examples of having hope in the face of what the absolute experts in their fields were telling them was a hopeless situation. Consequently, hope was one of the first critical concepts to navigating adversity I learned in life.

My parents stood up to the monster in my muscles. They said they would "try anyway," and then, they did. There was no guarantee that their efforts would pay off. But they had to *believe* it could. See, that's the thing about hope. Hope is merely a belief that something is *possible*.

Sometimes there are ZERO indications that anything else could be, but it's about believing anyway. The future is a mystery. Not many of us are able to look ahead and see the future. So, if you can't see it, and can't confirm what is to be, why not believe in the best possible scenario? The worst thing that will happen is that you'll be disappointed IF the outcome isn't what you'd hoped for. And IF the outcome is a bad one, THEN, absolutely, grieve and feel the pain or the sadness, or whatever is appropriate. But please, don't presuppose pain and suffering. Even if ALL indications, ALL history, ALL the experts, or ALL the facts point to something bad occurring, if you can BELIEVE something else COULD be possible, you hold the power.

I have seen life change on a dime—for good and for bad. I believe that by having hope and by being unwavering in it, it can set off a chain-reaction of other events that actually DO produce a better outcome. If you have hope, you are thinking positively. That hope can seep into your decisions, your actions, your behavior, your words, your openness to options. All THOSE things, then, can affect the way others perceive you and your circumstances. It can change the way others interact with you and, can potentially, cause them to act in your favor.

I'm not talking about being delusional here, folks. Deal in facts, 100%, yes. But what I am saying is that in life, there are twists and turns, unseen forces. There are things people don't know. Outside factors and influences and inside factors and influences, in addition to any number of things that could potentially impact how something will play out. And yes, sometimes all the hoping in the world won't change what is to come, but dangit. Why not live in that hope and see what happens? Guaranteed, it'll be a more pleasant journey on the way to the destination, at a minimum. Don't let a foregone conclusion rob you of hoping for—and by extension, maybe getting—something better.

So, let's talk a bit about my mission for this book. We are all on our own journey through life, but there are universal concepts we all come up against—that suck. Things like illness, job loss, rejection, fear, loneliness. My mission here is talk about these things, and share how I've navigated them, which, I hope, will inspire you to think a little differently about the things in YOUR life that suck and how YOU navigate them. Because of the universal nature of these themes, my hope is to bridge the gap some may initially see existing between my experience and your experience.

Because I realize that, at a glance, some may see this book as one full of stories from MY life and some nice-sounding ideas that don't apply to you because you're not in a wheelchair. I know that not everyone who picks up this book will be in a wheelchair or will relate to being disabled. My story is not your story. #Truth. But I propose that we actually have a lot more in common than may initially meet the eye. Our challenges may be unique, but adversity is universal. The tools and strategies and pathways through it are universal. That is how I see it.

I also have a ridiculously massive desire for my pain not to have been in vain. I want there to be a purpose to it, and I believe one such purpose may just be to help you through whatever similar or alternate struggle you may be facing in your own life. Allow me to deconstruct...

The struggle is real. Isn't that what they say? Unfortunately, and I'm sorry to be a "Debbie-downer," stick with me and I WILL land this plane. Adversity is a certainty in life. I know. "Check-please!" But, that is precisely what I want to drive home here. One of the few commonalities between every single human on the planet is that every one of us will have struggles, challenges and yes, pain-in-the-ass-Tuesday's.

As we've thoroughly established now, for me, first and foremost, my primary challenge is my disability (secondarily, I have 1,000 other examples we'll get into later in this book that have made my life challenging). For you, maybe it's also a disability. Or maybe it's mental illness, job loss, abuse, financial problems, divorce, or a loved one who is sick. I could go on. We've all experienced things in our lives that make life harder, and that make us cry—we ALL have bad days.

Some of our struggles are generally the same (sickness, divorce, debt, etc.). Lots of them are generally the same, but then the story and the details are almost always different. Many of our challenges are wildly different from one another. That doesn't mean that we can't use the same tools, strategies, and mindsets to navigate them. Just because I am disabled, and you maybe have been unemployed for a year, doesn't mean you can't use what my disability has taught me, and vice-versa, to get through it.

As I started writing this book, I heard people say that the privilege they've lived with and the challenges they have faced feel insignificant compared to what I've endured. While I appreciate the credit, I never want someone to diminish what they've been through because they don't think it's "as bad as mine."

It's a tricky thing, comparison. I heard Oprah once say, "pain is pain." We can't compare it. And personally, I don't believe we *should* compare it. Comparison is dangerous territory. There are people who have endured things that are unimaginable, yes. Someone who survived the Holocaust, for example, is deserving of *massive* amounts of respect and admiration, the likes of which words have not been invented to describe. But, at the same time, what you've been through and what I've been through are still deserving of acknowledgement, respect, tears, time…

In addition, what may look unbearable to one person may actually not be so bad for another. We all have different capacities and thresholds for pain. The severity, the scale, the variety are all things that each individual has a different tolerance for. My mom always used to say, "If we took every single person's problems in the whole entire world and piled them up on a hill and then looked at them and said, 'choose,' we would all go running for our own problem(s)."

See, there is also something to be said for familiarity—the devil you know, so to speak. For me, I have always been in a wheelchair. It's all I've ever known, and I've built my life around it. I've gotten "used to it." Don't get me wrong, there is a lot about it that has sucked, but it hasn't destroyed me. It hasn't stopped me. It hasn't ruined me. But I also know there are disabled people out there who are angry every single day of their lives. The two of us may just have different tolerances and coping mechanisms for the same general situation (which could have a lot of unique factors contributing to how each of our generally-the-same situations manifest differently. I know, it's getting deep!).

And yes, there are definitely times when one person seems to carry far more than their fair share. I have a friend, a woman named Madison, who I interviewed for this book. She was JUST married when their house was flooded in Hurricane Harvey. Right after that, her father-in-law died from aggressive colon cancer and she had to support her husband through the loss of his father. Then, HER mother was diagnosed with breast cancer, and Madison was in a horrible car accident that totaled her car, and THEN, her dad *texted her* that he was divorcing her mom. She was 23 and a new bride when all this rained down on her. I mean, come on!

But Madison withstood the storm. It didn't break her, it didn't destroy her, or her marriage, or anything else. Today, she is one of the wisest, most soulful, joyful people I know—and I suspect that has something to do with all she's endured.

I also feel compelled to call out the fact that not all adversity is visible to the naked eye.

Some adversity is quite visible—like my disability. In other cases, we would never guess what someone is struggling with because you can't *see* it. Mental illness is a perfect example of that. Mental illness can be a devastating challenge in a person's life, but because you can't see it from the outside, you may not receive the support, the sympathy, the generosity I've actually received because people can *see* my disability. People may think you should be able to suck it up, or take a pill, or "behave," all because they can't see the chemical imbalances in a person's brain.

Is my problem, the devastation of having to sit in a wheelchair all day worse than the mentally ill person's problems because you can actually SEE mine? Maybe yes. Maybe no. Why compare? A problem is a problem. A challenge is a challenge. Hard is hard. Pain is pain.

As we move ahead to the next chapter and beyond, I am going to share things that are hard. They are things that, in my life, caused me pain (physical AND emotional), and caused me to cry more tears than I can count. I'll share things that made me feel shame. Things that terrified and frustrated and angered me. And best of all, I'll share things that made me laugh like a maniac out of the sheer ridiculousness of them. You might ask yourself, why the heck would she do this? Honestly, from the bottom of my heart and soul, I do it for you.

I do it because I see a need in our world. COVID shook us in ways we never imagined. The racial climate in our world is in chaos. People have been destroyed professionally, financially, medically, relationships have suffered, and lives have been lost.

It is not an indictment on our society, but from where I sit (pun-intended!) I think people right now need help seeing the "bright side." I think some even need permission to know that seeing the bright side is okay. I think we need a different perspective—we need encouragement to shift from limiting beliefs to growth mindsets, hope, and I think people need to be seen.

In the pages of this book, I will tell you how I have struggled. But I am also telling you as loudly as I know how, "I see YOUR struggle too. It matters. I care. There is a way through. And you have permission to be happy, despite your circumstances. And I'd like to help."

Chapter 1:
Disability and Illness

There are a lot of ways that being in a wheelchair sucks. As Elizabeth Barrett Browning might say, "Let me count the ways…"

I thought long and hard about how to approach this chapter; it's the elephant in the room. Though I told you the story of my diagnosis in the introduction, I felt it would be wrong to leave out disability and illness as a whole, universal thing unto itself that sucks. Because I can tell you with complete certainty that for anyone in the world with a disability or an illness, it does, in fact, suck. And while I know that not every person who picks up this book will have a disability or an illness, the likelihood you will know or love someone who does is pretty darn near certain. This category reaches far and wide. According to the Center for Disease Control and Prevention's (CDC's) website, there are 61 million adults in the United States with a disability, which means approximately one in four adults in the United States is living with a disability. Just to be sure my category is as universal as it can be, I'm including any disabled AND/OR ill individuals. That means, I'm looking at YOU, people who are in wheelchairs, amputees, people who are blind or deaf or have invisible illnesses like fibromyalgia, chronic fatigue syndrome, mental illness. It includes people with cancer, Parkinson's disease, heart disease, HIV/AIDS, and so on. So again, the chances that you ARE or that you KNOW and love one of these people—pretty good.

They ways that disability and illness suck are many, yes. It will also vary according to what your (or the person you are "adjacent to") specific illness or disability actually is. For some of us, it affects how our physical person feels day in and day out. Our energy levels, and chronic pain we live with. It can affect our access to the world. How we dress might be impacted (don't get me started on fashion that compliments a 100% seated position, you guys!). Self-esteem? Yup! It can affect our inclusion at work, and in social settings. Sometimes it hits us in the wallet. It can change our ability to engage in activities we want to engage in. My dad will confirm that I am a roller-coaster riding, zip-lining, thrill-seeker at heart, but my disabled adult body doth protest.

I could continue to give you a big laundry list of the ways it sucks for those affected for disability or chronic illness, but I thought instead, I'd share one story with you that began my journey in life as a disabled person with the *awareness* that I would be disabled forever. I was about four, I think.

I remember the day I realized I would never walk. I must have been watching *Cinderella* or something recently, because I started out the day thinking about my wedding. A Disney fan at an early age, the image my mini-self awoke with in the morning was characteristic of my age. I can still close my eyes and see it. It was me, walking down the aisle in a big, poufy, white wedding dress, all silk and sequins, looking like a Disney princess, toward my Prince Charming. There may-or-may-not have been bluebirds chirping about my head and shoulders…

As a Type-A problem-solver, even at that early age, envisioning this day as I sat in my wheelchair, I knew I needed a solution to the "walking part." I swear to you, around this time, I had ALSO seen something on television about someone in a wheelchair who had done some kind of extreme-rehab and, very dramatically, got up out of their wheelchair and walked down the aisle at their wedding. I have fuzzy pictures of the show, news story, or whatever it was in my mind. Now I couldn't tell you exactly who or what it was, but because I'd seen it, the wheels in my mind were turning.

So, the overly-simplified context I carried around in my mind told me my legs were only weak, that was all. Seeing how I was four and stuff, I was uneducated about the disease that put me in a wheelchair, and the solution was completely logical to me. Exercise. Like the person I'd seen on TV. That was the solution.

How it must have broken my parent's hearts later that day when I shared my dream with them, what I had seen on TV and how I was going to do the same thing. When they tried to talk me out of it and help me to see the reality of my situation, I told them I knew I could do it if I exercised harder—and by the time I got married, I would be strong enough to walk down the aisle. If the guy on TV could do it, so could I! This event had become incredibly important to me in this moment and I remember feeling the urgency (maybe because deep-down, I sensed the doubt) as I explained. I needed to believe this would work.

In some eloquent way, my parents tried to help me understand this was not a realistic goal. I heard what they were saying, and I was beginning to feel the dream slip away a little at a time. But I was desperate to keep my grip on it. I kept trying to convince them that maybe with crutches, I could do it. It seemed like a reasonable compromise, but again, they tried to reason with me.

Unconvinced and determined, I *knew* they were wrong. I needed to *show* them. I explained to my dad patiently (SO patiently—clearly, he just didn't get it!) and confidently, if he held me in a standing position at the side of my bed, I could hold on, he could let go, and he would see I could support myself and stand there.

Oy. All he could do was let me try.

So, in this wide-eyed little girl's room, sitting on the floor next to my white eyelet canopy bed, my dad picked me up easily to a standing position and stood behind me. I was so proud of myself and I told him, "See! I'm standing!" To which he replied, "I haven't let go yet."

I told him to let go, I stiffened my legs, preparing for victory and felt his hands reluctantly retreat. I felt the enormous weight on my legs for barely a second before they betrayed me, and I slid down the bed to the floor.

That day, the fantasy I shared with so many other little Disney-watching girls was shattered. The image of my wedding day, looking like a princess, was replaced with a picture of me rolling down the aisle in a wheelchair, which I still clung to, but somehow didn't hold the magic its predecessor had.

It was the day I gave in. Not gave-UP, mind-you, but the day I gave in. Though I was too young to fully understand all the implications this disease would have on the structure of my life, something inside me felt the trap shut. Buckle-up, Buttercup—here we go…

The truth about things that suck is, well, they suck. Adversity comes in all kinds of shapes and sizes, and may look different to everyone, but the very definition of adversity suggests, it's going to suck. If you are ill, if you have a disability as I do, or you know someone who does, then you know—it sucks.

Adversity, in general, is a challenge in your life that is typically accompanied by a slew of natural responses and emotions that make us feel bad. And I believe that it is super-important to acknowledge that right off the bat. Things that suck…SUCK. So, I want to begin by acknowledging that FOR you and I want to reassure you that it's okay, and I'll tell you why.

We all have the friend who immediately goes to pushing the bright side on us as soon as something goes wrong. I've *been* that friend. And (don't get me wrong) I will STILL be the first to tell you (when the time is right) that finding the bright side is critical. But what I know *now* is that sometimes, we JUST need to sit with something that qualifies as "bad" for a minute and claim the suck. And we need to be allowed to say it out loud, if for no other reason than because it's true.

If I think back to being a kid and a teenager, I can remember distinctly NOT wanting to hear why maybe my disability was a blessing of some sort, in disguise. Nope—I was a kid and I was lonely, and that SUCKED and I wanted someone to tell me that I was right. I wanted that very real part of my life and those very real feelings to be *seen* and to be okay. On top of all the sucking of the situation, I didn't want to have to feel WRONG for feeling the way I did.

I think that, kind of like an alcoholic who professes that they ARE an alcoholic as part of the healing process, accepting that something bad sucks is healthy. It squares us in reality, it validates the feelings we are having, and it communicates to us and to others that our brains and our hearts are doing battle with something unpleasant…something frustrating…maybe even something devastating. And that *that* needs some time to process. I am not a psychologist, but I know in situations where something bad has happened, grieving and feeling our emotions is important.

But an interesting thing happened. After spending 40-something years getting really, really good at navigating MY adversity, and as I pivoted to becoming a motivational speaker and a writer who spends ALL their time teaching people how to navigate adversity well and how to pull as much of the good from it as we can, and how to use it to our advantage, I lost sight of the VERY FIRST STEP in it all—letting it suck.

I had the honor to interview Shawn Achor, happiness researcher and author of the best-selling book ***The Happiness Advantage*** and he reminded me that people need to hear that "It's ok to not be ok" for a minute. In fact, now I also wonder, if we numb ourselves, and don't let ourselves feel and connect to the broken bits that go along with adversity, we may never develop that reinforcing scar that makes us stronger and more resilient going forward. Food for thought.

So, now that we all have permission to acknowledge and to sit with the negative feelings for a while, there IS a second truth about things that suck—they won't suck forever.

Let me say that again for the people in the back. Things won't suck forever. AND, not everything about life has to suck, just because part of it does.

As we move forward through this book together, there are a lot of ideas, strategies, tools, and stories of my own AND from others I have to share with you that will take us on a journey out of the darkness and back into the light, but for now, let's just look at the mere existence of adversity in our world and come to terms with what the actual heck it is and why we might need it in our lives.

According to Merriam-Webster, adversity is a "a state or instance of serious or continued difficulty or misfortune." A few of the synonyms for adversity are, "misfortune," "tragedy," and "misadventure." Like I said, it's going to suck.

As we consider why we need adversity in the world, or why the presence of adversity serves a purpose, let's go to the extreme and imagine that we have the power to eliminate any and all bad things in the world. For grins, let's consider a world where nothing bad ever happens, for just a second. I feel a bit like Clarence in "It's a Wonderful Life" (cue wind and snow...).

Think about a perfect world—utopia. Everyone has a roof over their heads, food on their tables, perfect health, abundant bank accounts, family, friends, etc. I'm not going to lie—sometimes, this sounds like the EXACT world I want to live in. But then, to play devil's advocate, let me ask you a few questions:

1. If we never saw a person with no home, how could we feel grateful for our own?
2. If we never knew or saw a person with a disability or battling a serious illness, how could we feel compassion?
3. If we never gave our time, our money, or our blood to victims of natural disaster, how could we know generosity?

The truth is that the bad exists to define the good, and vice versa. Without the bad, how could we ever recognize the good? Without the bad, the world would be just a superficial acceptance of gifts, with no real meaning or significance to them. The challenges that we endure, and that we watch each other endure culminates in a world full of people who are grateful and compassionate and generous.

THAT is the world I want to live in. Unfortunately, to live in that world, you have to take the bad (like a disability or an illness) along with the good.

It's become a cliche to say that adversity is one of the most character-building gifts we receive. But (as someone, somewhere said) a cliche becomes a cliche for a reason. It's SO true that it is said over and over and over again. But if you look at what I said a moment ago, the generosity, the compassion and the gratitude that the bad things expose to us, these are some of the characteristics that are cultivated in us as we either experience or observe adversity. And, it occurs to me that some of our finest qualities are actually found in times of adversity.

But there is another facet to the question of "why." My explanation above is pretty general and pretty universal. And assuming that we can all agree to the theory that adversity serves to provide definition, significance and meaning to the good things in life, and that adversity brings forth characteristics in us that are, arguably, the most valuable, the other piece I have to suggest to you is more individualized. Here it is. When we ask "why" bad things happen, I say, the "why" is on us.

Hold on, hear me out—please don't snap the book shut. It may feel like me putting the own-ness back on you to figure out the answer to this question is a cop-out, or a way of even re-victimizing you, and your first instinct may be to demand a refund. Give it a chance to sink in, though.

I've lived 40-something years, hoping that *someone* would give me a magical answer to this question. Something that would explain my disability and cancer and earthquakes and mass shootings and terrorist attacks. And, in all that time, I have yet to hear an answer that rings true or that comes close to making sense of it all.

Now, while I DO believe, strongly, in fact, that adversity DOES give meaning and significance to the good things we experience in life and the blessings we receive, I don't believe that this is THE one, all-encompassing, broad-sweeping answer for all of it. That would be far too simplistic, and to be honest, it's a good start, but not good enough to explain why a woman named Sally, a young, married mother of two who I interviewed for this book survived breast cancer, only to get stomach cancer, and then die of a brain hemorrhage mid-way through her treatment.

Honestly, if we each take on the "why," WE get to be in control. And there is power, and more significant meaning to be found in that. WE get to decide why. WE get to assign meaning to the adversity we walk through and observe. WE get to find the purpose.

You may be thinking, "Great—more work. After I've already gone through this terrible time of suffering, NOW you want me to dig in and figure out what it all meant??" Yes, I do.

Because, notice—I said "get to" in each of those statements above. I DIDN'T say "have to." You *don't* have to, but you *do* GET to. From that standpoint, that *very slight* shift in perspective, maybe you can look at it as an honor rather than a burden? And, honestly, isn't it BETTER for there to be some meaning or some bigger purpose to it all than for it just to remain forever in our minds some terrible thing that just happened and that we had to get over?

You may be thinking, "Thanks, but no thanks. I'm tired. That sucked. And, I'm done." I believe *wholeheartedly* that if we don't do this work to look for the "why," (whether we do the looking during or after) we are in danger of becoming bitter. We may become jaded, or become angry people. I've seen it. I've seen it in others, AND when I have failed to spend a minute looking for meaning in MY adversity, I've seen it in myself.

Years ago, I spent several months as sort of a prisoner in my home. See, I was born a living, breathing contradiction—a person with a fiercely independent nature, but who is shackled to a wheelchair, has limited physical abilities, and who is dependent on people day in and day out to get me out of bed, help me bathe, etc.

During this time, the car I drove (a car that is super-duper high tech, built to my exact specifications, and took a year and $130,000 to build) was showing its age and had to be sent to another city to be worked on because your standard auto shops and mechanics don't work on this kind of car. I was in Austin, and the car had to go to Houston.

The repairs were expensive, and the funding for it was complicated, to say the least, and the months dragged on. Meanwhile, the city I lived in had limited public transportation options, and I couldn't just rent any car at any rental place. So, I stayed home. For months. Not able to get to work, to drive my seven-year old daughter around. Nothing. I worked from home, fearing all the time that my job was in jeopardy because I couldn't get to the office.

Then, one day, BOTH of my personal care assistants quit. On the same day. The people who got me in and out of bed, dressed, bathed, etc. Do you know how I found that out? The one who was to show up to get me out of bed that morning never came and never answered my calls again. And when I called the other one to see if she could come and help, she said she was unavailable and, in fact, had some personal issues and wasn't going to be able to come back at all. Wait, what?! Yup.

I spent days-on-end in my pajamas because I was having to rely on my husband to get me in and out of bed and I didn't want to have to ask him for MORE care. (Let me be clear—he'd have done it. But when we married, because of my naivety and my independent streak, I'd told him I wanted a husband, not a nurse, and that we should keep those two things separate.)

So, suddenly, 98% of what I had spent years architecting to be that fiercely independent woman was gone. The entire house of cards shattered. I felt like a failure as a mother, as a wife and partner, as an employee…as a human. I felt like a burden. And I began to get bitter, and angry, and to feel like it was ALL for nothing, and like I should just stop fighting against what I was—a broken, physically UNABLED person. Seriously. Those were my thoughts. I had very little faith left in anything. And it scared me. I saw a glimpse of what I *could* become, and I didn't like it.

That is what happens when the glow of hope begins to dim. Fortunately, I recognized it when it started to happen. I knew I didn't want to live in my head with THOSE thoughts for the rest of my life. I didn't want to be the person who was so miserable and defeated that I didn't even want to be in my OWN company.

I am someone who has always had a belief in a higher power and had believed I was here for a reason. I called my minister, told him what was happening and told him that I was losing my faith and needed help.

He came, of course, and we talked. And, he HEARD me. And he was so sorry I was going through what I was, and just that conversation lightened the load, and I began the process to find hope again. I had a bit more time to deal with my situation, but then I hired new assistants (and

I'm not going to SAY that the other two had done me a favor and that these two new assistants ended up being two of my all-time FAVORITE assistants, but…), and my car was sent back to me, and life went on—me, my fiercely independent self, and I.

I think that, in order to avoid becoming people we never wanted to be in response to a blow, we need to make that shift at the right time from "appreciating" the suckiness of the situation, to being purposeful and intentional about looking for a healthier mindset, meaning, or a lesson, or a purpose. Eventually, you have to move into problem solving mode. And now, in retrospect, I can also see that there was a purpose to all this. New people who I cherish even today (twelve years later) came into my life for a season. But even if I couldn't see the purpose then I knew that the persona I was living wasn't who I wanted to keep show up as until my problems were resolved.

Sometimes, life pummels us. And if we don't find constructive ways to look at the rocks we're being hit with, we can become the very worst version of ourselves. A version no one else will want to be around, and ultimately, maybe a person even YOU don't want to be around.

Where does that leave you?

In my own life, I've watched other people who I love turn from being open, optimistic, happy people to people who expect bad things to happen to them and to other people. It doesn't always happen overnight, but it WILL happen. Ever heard of a self-fulfilling prophecy? If you're looking for it, if you're expecting it, it will show up for you every single time. Good or bad. So why not spend your time looking for, expecting and receiving the good?

I could look at my disability as a curse. There are days when *I have*. It could be this bleak, painful, limiting thing that *happened to me* to make my life hard, that makes me a challenge to go on social outings with, and an outsider who is different from everyone I know. I could see it as something that causes others who don't know any better to underestimate my capabilities. I could see myself as a burden. And I could see an ugly physical form that can't exercise, and that has atrophied over years of non-use. It would be SO easy to let those be my only thoughts.

Because here's the thing—if I look at what I wrote in that paragraph above, some of those statements are true. They are. They might be unfortunate, but they ARE true. I AM a challenge to go on social outings with. There are extra considerations and logistics to consider. Accessibility is a real consideration and there are a lot of activities that are eliminated as options because I can't do them or because the places where they occur are inaccessible. It's just a fact. I am also A RIOT and so much stinking fun to hang out with, you wouldn't know what hit you. That is also true.

I AM different from almost everyone I know. Truth. But then, so are you—maybe for a different reason, but you ARE different. My muscles HAVE atrophied over the years and I can't exercise. That's true—however, it's mixed with the untruth that it makes me ugly. This is where our minds play dirty tricks on us, and we weave together these complicated stories full of truths overshadowed by untruths and it all has the *potential* to become very negative.

Because, you see, it is possible to have multiple realities that are different, but that are both true at that same time. In my conversation with Mr. Achor, we talked about the idea that when we are sitting in a place of hurt or of anger, and that the very real circumstances that caused those feelings become one part of your reality, sometimes that creates a shadow over anything else in our world that is good—our family, our kids, our jobs, our health, our furry-faced pets, just to name a few. Those are potential things that ALSO exist in our realities that are positive. Once we begin to see those things again and remember the meaning they hold for us, the negative diminishes—maybe very slightly at first—but nevertheless, it gives us truth to believe in that is more than just our sucky adversity.

Why is it so much easier to sit in anger, frustration, and sadness? Because taking something so inherently negative and turning it into something positive requires *effort*. Changing the nature of something requires work, thought, and then perseverance and consistency to keep it that way. Work, thought, perseverance, and consistency? Yes, it's exhausting. But OMG, so worth it when you find out that you're a badass capable of something so hard. And it IS hard at first, but it's a muscle. The more you do it, the easier, more natural and second-nature it becomes.

Every day, I wake up with a body that is broken and weighted by atrophied muscles. Finding anything to be grateful for or to appreciate about my body is impossible some days.

BUT, on the days when I realize all I've accomplished *despite* the fight my body puts up every day, I feel proud and grateful to my body for pushing me to see what I AM capable of. When I sit on a stage and talk to an audience of people about my broken body and the things I've done despite my body's lack of cooperation, and then I get to see the motivation or the gratitude in someone else's face who's realized *the alternative* to their ability to walk on the treadmill or run up the stairs, and I know that MY body was the example that revealed why their thighs are actually pretty amazing? I am proud.

It still sucks that my thighs are WAY un-toned and jiggly. It would be SO MUCH more fun to have thighs like Jennifer Lopez, but the truth is, I DON'T have Jennifer Lopez's thighs. Few of us do—amiright?? But, if I am open and intentional, I CAN see the purpose of *my* thighs, and that changes <u>everything</u> about how I feel about them.

I've heard so many examples of other people, too, who have experienced devastation or loss or traumatic experiences. Normal, everyday people like me, who have gone on to take their adversity and use it (whether intentionally or by accident) as a powerful force in someone else's life.

I interviewed an amazing woman named Pvamela for this book. She went through eight years of infertility issues. Eight years of treatments and of experimenting and of hope and disappointment. Eight years of out-of-control hormones and emotions, injections and IVF procedures. All those years of feeling like a failure once a month—feeling like a failure 96 times, you guys. One of the things that helped her through it was a support group for women facing infertility issues. In the end, she took over leading that support group and, over time, managed to help hundreds of women going through the same exact trauma she was going through.

I credit some of my worst days with so many of my best qualities—qualities that my struggles instilled in me—strength, courage, determination, ambition, perseverance, creativity, and a sense of humor. These are the same qualities I needed to employ in my life in order to accomplish almost every goal I've ever attempted. And I have.

Guys, the pain will be. So, let it be. Some pain will be worse than others. You may experience mini-pain and/or macro-pain. His pain may appear worse than her pain. You can't compare.

It doesn't matter what your adversity is. During or after, ask yourself, what is this/did this teach me? Did it drive my life in this direction, toward this outcome instead of that one? How did it make me better? How did it make SOMEONE ELSE better? I know for an absolute fact that some of the crummy cards I've been dealt have been intended to serve as examples for someone else. That is not always a fun position to find yourself in, to have to go through pain and suffering so someone else can learn a lesson, but it's powerful if you get to watch it unfold. But—hear me on this—you have to LET YOURSELF see it unfold.

One final word on our "why." Stop fighting the "why." Be honest, sometimes we know what it is, and we fight against it because we're angry. Or we don't like it. We want to be mad. We get caught up in or addicted to the drama, and we want the injustice to have been so great that there can't possibly be a "why." We just want to have been wronged.

How does that anger serve you? Look for a reason anyway. Acknowledge it anyway. What's that old saying? "You don't have to believe it, but it doesn't mean it's not true?" Even if you deny it, the "why" may still stand. So, let yourself take comfort in it.

I believe that any challenge we experience, regardless of what it is, can teach us patience or courage or grace. Or all of the above. If I can't find any other reason, I can find peace in *that*. When you look for a reason—when you ALLOW there to be a reason—it softens the blow. It lessens the sting of adversity. Give yourself that gift. I'll say it again. Repeat this to yourself five times today.

The truth about things that suck is...they SUCK. The second truth is, it won't suck forever. Bonus truth! If you look for it, you can find a purpose for it and define the sucking.

Chapter 2:
Fear

Where do I even begin? I am sitting in fear right this second. I wish I were kidding, but I have been staring at my computer screen for 50 minutes, unsure how to write the next chapter. NO WORDS were coming. I've been alternating between looking at a blank page, looking through the outline of my book over and over again, hoping inspiration would strike to write ANY one of the chapters in the outline. I've been Googling key words from my chapter titles, hoping that somehow, somewhere I would read something that would trigger a powerful memory, or that I would come across a compelling quote, or even a song lyric that could get me started. I have a list of stories from my life in my book outline that could serve to illustrate any of these "things that suck," but I've been lacking the right inspiration to tell them in the most compelling ways.

I'm terrified that nothing I write will be good enough. This book is such a huge dream of mine; I've been sitting here, putting so much pressure on myself to make it great that I couldn't bring myself to write a single word for fear that the words I choose won't measure up.

I've been thinking about my writing deadline, and all the what-if's. What if I can't come up with anything to write today? And what if that bleeds over into tomorrow, and what if I get down to having only three weeks left to my deadline and I still have, say, 15 chapters to write? What if I just don't have enough to say and I never complete this book, and all the time, work and effort over the last 10 years it took me to get a publishing contract were for nothing and this dream actually DOESN'T come true after all? Ah, the destructive loops that play in our minds, yes? The self-imposed pressure that takes us to the darkest possible places creating fictitious sabotage and failure of our goals, dreams and entire futures, leaving us with no security and no solutions, THUS, resulting in deeper and deeper levels of fear.

It hit me—I am sitting, in real-time, in the middle of one of my self-professed "things that suck." And suddenly, the writer's block has dissolved.

Fear shows up for us in so many different ways, shapes and forms. There is "real" fear…like a tiger chasing you, or maybe a more likely example, being in a car accident. There is also what I'm going to call conjured or manufactured fear. Like I've been experiencing for the past hour. Both can be equally threatening in our mind's eye, though, can't they? Our bodies have the same response, regardless of whether the danger is real or conjured.

Let's talk for just a second about this manufactured fear. The fear of the unknown. The fear of the "what if's?" in life. The fear we create from insecurity, and doubt that leads to a complete undoing (in our minds) of our life, our safety, our livelihood…

How much time do you spend making up futures that may-or-may-not ever occur? We tell ourselves stories about things that are to come that are not grounded in any kind of reality. What if I get fired? What if it's cancer? What if my husband is having an affair and leaves me? What if my child falls off their bicycle and breaks their leg?

Do you know what's funny about my writing "what if's?" I do this almost every time I write something—a blog post, an article, a chapter for this book. It's almost become this little self-destructive piece of my creative process. Most of the time, I actually DO realize what I am doing. I realize the familiarity of what I am doing, AND then become aware of the history that tells me—I always come up with something. Yet, when my brain is stuck in this loop, imagining the bad things that are going to happen and that my career as a writer is about to be over, because I am definitely not going to be able to come up with the words *this time*, I feel like I almost may as well get eaten by the metaphorical tiger that is chasing me, because that is the kind of panic and terror that rises up in me.

Why do we do this to ourselves??? Because what I've come to realize it that so much of the severity level of the things in our worlds that suck is brought on by a flawed mindset about them. Read that again—I'll wait.

Because what I've realized over years of life is that so many things that suck in our lives could suck a lot less if we looked at them with a mindset of openness, hope, and flexibility. We have so much more control over how bad things get than we think we do, when we own the way we think about them. I'm not a mental health professional—but I have my own theories that make sense to me, and solutions or strategies for navigating these things that have worked for me, and that I hope will work for you.

In this case, I'm thinking about how fear threatens our basic human needs. If you are familiar with Maslow's hierarchy of needs, then you know that this theory builds a foundation of the most basic needs of every human to function and to live. Safety/security is one of those basic human needs. And, fear is the threat to our safety. And, voila!

When we are uncertain of something, insecure about something, are in unfamiliar territory, or have a problem we don't yet know how to solve, it makes some sense to me that our minds will try to decipher the messiness for us. AND it makes sense that the most natural tendency might be to jump to worrying about, and "pre-protecting" ourselves against any threat to our most basic needs that this uncertainty or problem may present if we can't fix or solve it.

Now, what do we do about it, though?

In the case of conjured or manufactured fear, I think awareness is a great start. Being able to stop and realize when your mind is spinning in all sorts of directions that (at this point in time) have not happened and may never happen, is critical. In my writing example, it's true that a point came when I became aware that my brain was telling me stories about things that were actually unlikely to happen. I recognized my pattern and that rational side kicked in and made space for the panic to calm and for more constructive thoughts and ideas to flow.

In some situations, awareness is enough to stop the panic and the anxiety that ensues right away for me. Sometimes, the awareness needs time to breathe and percolate and make its way through all the tall tales before it can calm our worries.

What I can tell you though, is that for me, being aware of the loop and the not-yet-true stories is *always* enough to calm me down so I can refocus the way I am thinking about something. Sometimes, I have to try several new ways of thinking. At times, I have to leave what I'm doing and create some kind of distraction to fully pull my mind out of the loop and come back to what I'm doing later when I've gotten some space from the "loop of fear." But eventually, awareness wins and my mind will finally concede that this is only a *possibility* that I am making up and that I still have all kinds of influence over what is to come.

But what about real fear? What about those times when we are experiencing a real and present threat? What about those of you (us) who have faced fear caused by losing our job, or terminal illness, bankruptcy or any number of other very serious, real-life scenarios that create very real fear in us?

The way I see it, the same basic premise is true—there is some threat that is presenting itself and jeopardizing our heath or personal safety or security. But when it is real, there is no rationalization that this is something that we are making up or that it may actually never come true. It's here.

About 12 years ago, I was in a baaaad car accident. As a type-A overachiever, when I do something, I go all in, and boy did I ever.

I was driving home after having just dropped my daughter off at soccer practice (and can I just say, "thank goodness, because she wasn't with me when it happened!"). It was dusk and I was about a mile away from home (which incidentally is, I hear, where they say a very large percentage of accidents happen) and was driving on a windy country road, one lane in each direction, no shoulders. Just grass and trees and brush to the sides of the road, and the speed limit was 55 mph. I was obeying traffic rules and driving 55 mph.

Suddenly, up ahead, in the middle of my lane, looking straight at me was a tiny, baby deer, standing perfectly still and giving no signs that it would be moving out of my lane or off the road.

Now, I don't know about you, but I don't always make the right choice in split-second decisions. There were options—I could have stopped very suddenly, but that may have caused the car behind me to slam into me and even more people could have been injured. I could have hit the deer, but I am a bleeding-heart animal lover and I don't think any cell in my body was going to let that happen ever in this lifetime.

Nope. I swerved. And when I swerved, I went off the road and lost control of my car and barreled 55 mph into a super-sturdy, well-rooted, unmoving tree.

Spoiler alert—the outcome of the accident was a broken right wrist that required surgery to fix, and TWO broken femurs requiring two months of hospitalization AND 27 stitches to a crazy-nasty gash in my right leg below the knee that has left me with a pretty gnarly scar. Like I said, if I'm going to do something, I don't half-ass it!

It was serious, folks. But I can report—the sweet, little doe-eyed asshat lived.

So, apart from the fear that hit immediately before, during and after the accident, I had a deeper fear that I couldn't shake for months. As we've established, I am in a wheelchair. I have a progressive condition and TERRIBLE bone-density because I don't walk and put daily stress and pressure on my bones to reinforce them. I *already* had limited movement and flexibility and range-of-motion.

Side note that will tell you something about my personality—as the paramedics rolled me into the ER on a stretcher (with LOTS of pain-killers rolling through my bloodstream by then), I remember being SO dismayed that none of the healthcare workers bustling around the ER would smile at me. Everyone was SO serious and in my frightened state…I really wanted someone to smile back at me. At that point, because of the lack of smiling, I was sure my broken legs and broken wrist must be fatal. And everyone knew it. Maybe it was the pain medicine talking, but I was smiling—why shouldn't they?! Anyway…

I had no idea how or IF my body was going to recover from this accident, and no one else could tell me what I might be looking at long-term. My recovery and the techniques the doctors and physical therapists used were not going to be able to look like an able-bodied person's. We were making it up as we went along. Best case scenario, one of my orthopedists told me it would be a year before my legs would heal, and as for when the pain would subside—never, maybe? Or maybe in six weeks. Ugh. All the other things? Flexibility, range of motion, etc. Who knows?

Fear is one of those things that, well—I don't know many people who respond to fear well. Personally, I can be calm and pragmatic in business situations, or in another person's crisis, but when something is affecting me medically—probably because of my already complicated medical circumstances—AND my fiercely independent nature and the lengths I've gone to in order to overcome my medical/physical circumstances and to live a relatively normal and independent life—when you threaten THAT, I'll just say, it takes me a minute to enhance my calm. When something threatens my independence, that is my everything.

Whether I could have articulated it back in those moments or not, what I've learned is this. And this is not a small thing, guys. There is a big difference between fear and courage. You can be afraid and STILL be brave and courageous. In fact, it's the act of being courageous in the face of fear that MAKES us brave.

During the two months I spent in the hospital, I was afraid. Every time someone came into my hospital room, I wasn't sure if they were coming to give me news I didn't want to hear, or to make me do something that was going to hurt at a level of 14 on a scale from 1-10, or if they needed to stick me with another needle.

I did the only thing I could. I took the next step. Every. Single. Time. I woke up every morning to a painful, tedious, and un-fun schedule of physical and occupational therapy, and medicine and getting up and down from bed into my wheelchair with two broken femurs. I talked to the doctors and the nurses. I ate the disgusting hospital food (OMG, the food was DISGUSTING! One happy side-effect—I lost 20 pounds in two months because the food was sooooo disgusting.). Minute-by-minute and day-by-day, I did what came next. I tried not to think about what came after that. I focused on the task before me, and I cried when I felt like crying. I woke up every next morning deciding to do it all again—whether it hurt, or terrified me—to do it anyway. Even though I didn't know what the outcome was going to be, and that fear lived as a constant in the back of my mind—whether I would heal properly and regain all the function I had, and get past the pain—but I knew all I could do was to keep going.

Navigating fear is largely about choices. I knew, for example, that if I didn't do the physical therapy, and got sent home by my insurance company because I wasn't complying with the recommended treatment, it was a certainty that I would not regain my flexibility and strength. I didn't know that the painful, sucky physical and occupational therapy WAS going to restore everything, but I KNEW if I didn't do it, that I for sure wouldn't get better. So, I played the odds. I hoped for the best. I made peace with having to do things that hurt and that I didn't want to do. I chose courage and I chose the hard work that didn't guarantee me a perfect outcome but that was the best shot I had at it. I also got to brag to my friends and coworkers that I was "hitting the gym" (a.k.a., going to physical and occupational therapy) and working out twice a day. Slight exaggeration, but I'd earned it!

There is a great quote by Mandy Hale that I cite all the time, "It's ok to be scared. Being scared means you're about to do something really, really brave." For me, one of the biggest compliments someone can pay me is to call me brave. There is so much about my physical circumstances that can threaten my independence, my relationships, my work, my finances, because of the fragility of my physical health. I had a doctor once who observed that for me to be out and about on my own, day in and day out, doing the things any other person would do (going to work, running errands, meeting a friend for coffee), puts me at a higher risk should something go wrong.

But I'm unwilling to compromise my quality of life, to *give in* to the fear that may be present, and stop living the way it is in my nature to live so that nothing bad will ever happen. Every day, I have to wake up and renew my commitment to be brave and to live and to do hard things, because THAT is the life I want to lead. Does it mean I don't get exhausted by it? Nope. I just do it anyway.

So, what about you? What are YOU afraid of? Are your fears real and looking you in the eye, or are they manufactured fears and stories you are telling yourself about what *might* happen? It doesn't matter what your answer is, by the way—I'll accept either one, because remember what I said? Whether real or imagined, these fears create the same kind of anxiety and stress and emotion in our minds and in our bodies. The fear is valid, and it is okay to be afraid. I only ask so you will get into the habit of asking the question yourself—"Is this real, or is it a story I am making up?"

I do want to say one other quick thing. I hear the other objection you may be making—"Well, so maybe this hasn't happened yet, but it's going to. It just is. It's the only possible way this could play out." To that, I say, "You may be right. But what if you're not." Yes, sometimes the writing is on the wall, sometimes the odds are stacked against us and sometimes we believe we've exhausted all our options. You can still choose to live in hope. Like I said in the first chapter, hope is powerful stuff, and if you *believe* that something is even the tiniest bit possible, it can affect your behavior, your choices, someone else's choices—any slew of other things. And maybe it won't, but let it be *possible*!

I know that there are an infinite number of things that may be causing fear in you today—an illness, a difficult conversation you need to have with a boss or a loved one, financial issues, divorcing and starting a life over, unemployment, the safety of your children, etc. Make sure you are fearing what is real, and if you aren't, let the awareness of what you might be making up remind you that this is something that hasn't happened yet, and that you still may have some control over so why not breathe a little until it actually does while you spend your energy thinking positive thoughts that may influence how you go about trying to manipulate the outcome. Those positive thoughts may open you up to a whole host of subtle options and nuances to how you approach things that may change *everything*.

And if you are going through something scary, let me say that I am so very sorry. It sucks, I know. I may not know what your specific circumstance is, but what I *do know* is that we are almost always stronger than our circumstances. I hear people say all the time, "Oh, I could never handle that!" But you know what? You could. If you had to. If you had that scary thing looking you in the eye, you COULD handle it, because honestly, what choice do we have? We survive or we don't. It's true that what doesn't kill us makes us stronger. You can handle so much more than you think you can, so be brave, and take another step. It's okay to be afraid. Just don't let it stop you from being brave.

Chapter 3:
Failure

I never became a country music singing sensation. From the time I was about six, I was positive that I would. I'm going to date myself, and if you didn't follow country music in 1979…well, first of all, I feel sad for you, and second of all, put your seatbelt on because music from 1979 and a dream to be a country music star makes for a good story.

Back in the late '70s or early '80s, Barbara Mandrell was dominating the country music charts, winning all the "Entertainer of the Year" awards and had her own show on Saturday nights on primetime TV called "Barbara Mandrell & the Mandrell Sisters." Holy cats, did I ever live for Saturday nights!

I was learning around this time that I really, really liked music, and she was so dynamic and fun to watch—she and her sisters would sing and dance these crazy dance numbers and get thrown in the air by cowboys, doing these magnificent acrobatic dance numbers. The music was catchy and fun and there was nothing I didn't love about Barbara Mandrell.

I had ALL her records, and yes, I'm talking vinyl (if you are younger than 35 years old, Google vinyl and record players). I spent HOURS in my room, playing her songs over and over and over again, learning the music, memorizing the lyrics, trying to match her tone and intonation. I was pretty sure that I was going to grow up to be her best friend and sing alongside her on her show. In fact, people started to tell me, even at seven or eight years old, that I was rather good. That was allllll I needed to hear. Game on!

Let me digress for a second and revisit the borne contradiction within me because it's particularly relevant in this story.

Whoever created me (I, personally, believe in God and in a power bigger than myself) had a top-notch sense of humor. I was created with significant physical limitations that make me physically dependent on people, but I have a **fiercely** independent spirit.

That contradiction in me ignited the heart of a dreamer (and a daredevil, which *isn't* relevant to this story, but follows the train of thought, and—as I've said before—I LOVE a good roller-coaster!). I think my disability created certain gaps in me where the things might have lived that I couldn't do and the experiences I couldn't have been a part of—dance, athletics—anything physical were absent. And because of my nature, my quest for independence and my "dreamer" tendencies were magnified and I looooonged to fill these gaps with things that were exceptional, like becoming a country music singing sensation. Even at the age of eight, I had a voracious work ethic and spent hours upon hours singing to Barbara's records from behind the door of my bedroom, belting out "Sleeping Single in a Double Bed," which I can only imagine was beyond traumatizing for my parents who could only let it happen (remember, I was eight. What did I know about sleeping single or what the size of the bed was and why one might lament having the extra space??).

So, I sang—every chance I could get. I sang in the church choir. I sang and competed in high school. Then I went to college and got…distracted by independence and sorority life and all the things that were so new to me. Suffice it to say, I lost sight of music in favor of other things, and my grades in college weren't great. #didntquitefail.

Once I graduated college, though, and had spent a little time figuring out how to adult, I started to remember this dream I'd had. And I got to work. I got the attention of a music producer in Austin and he began working with me. I sang on the national Muscular Dystrophy Association's Jerry Lewis telethon three times (the third time, I got to sing an original song I'd gotten from a Texas songwriter, with the telethon's 40-piece orchestra at CBS studios in Los Angeles. It was one of the biggest and best moments of my life). I recorded a 3-song demo with George Strait's musicians, y'all! I sang in the famous SxSW music festival in Austin, TX. Things were going well, and I was gaining some traction.

I spent a bunch of time researching who represented some of my favorite country musicians—their agents and their labels—and I began sending out demos to them. Then, I started getting rejections. Now, I KNOW, making it in music is h-a-r-d. I probably needed to move to Nashville if I was going to have a real shot at it, but I didn't see a way to make that happen (financially, AND for me, moving and living logistics with caretakers and all that jazz seemed overly daunting) and I didn't believe it was anything ANYONE in my life would have approved of (Did I ask them? Of course not! I just made up stories I *thought* would be true). I was still only 26 years old, and I didn't really have the confidence to do something I didn't have complete and utter support to do. And since I didn't ask for their support, I 100% for sure didn't feel like I had it—or, could ever get it.

And then, the fear began to kick in. I continued telling myself stories that matched my new need to play it safe. I was old enough and had been adulting long enough to know that having a disability is expensive. I knew I needed to be at a certain income level to be able to take care of my needs, and I wanted to be comfortable, not just get by. And so, even though I had this producer who believed in me, and I was doing some cool things and getting a bit of traction, I stopped. No, that's not what happened. I didn't stop; I quit.

I QUIT, Y'ALL! I started getting rejections, and I realized how much work it was going to be and that there were no guarantees. (Umm, duh?) It was risky. And, I told myself I wasn't getting any younger, and that I needed to choose. I had thought about going back to grad school for a master's degree—partly to make up for the terrible showing I had in my undergraduate work, and partly to create security for my future and to open doors in my corporate career. I had a brilliant friend and mentor at the time who made me believe that I was smart enough to get into grad school and do the hard work to get a master's, and the allure of *that* success in the face of a dicey music career was strong.

I didn't believe at the time that I could have both. I thought I had to choose one or the other (spoiler alert—that was a LIE!). And I was scared (wish I'd read my chapter back then on "Fear," so I'd have known then that I could be both afraid AND brave). Ultimately, I chose the more certain path. I called the producer, told him I appreciated all he had done for me, but that I needed to be sure I had some security going forward, and that I was going back to school. He was gracious and kind, but I can only imagine now what a slap in the face that must have been to him after all the time and energy he'd invested in me.

Of course, I could have done both! I was so young and so wrapped up in fear that I sabotaged myself. Now, I'm not saying I would have been the next Barbara Mandrell, after-all, but what if I could have? What if I could have been the first commercially successful country music singer in a wheelchair? What if I could have just kept singing and making local people in Austin, TX happy? What if I'd kept singing and made *myself* happy? What if. What if's suck, people.

So, let's talk about *true* failure. Spoiler alert, I don't believe many things in life are *true* failures. I believe most of the things we see as failures are really redirections, or learning opportunities. So many of the things we see as failures, I've decided may be more appropriately labeled as disappointments. Maybe even setbacks. In this case, the *true* failure here wasn't that I never became a country music singing sensation. If there WAS a failure in this scenario, it was that I quit something I loved and that I gave in to fear. Is it failure or regret, though? Or a learning experience? When I first began planning how to write this chapter, in my mind, the failure was that I quit and that I will always wonder how far I might have been able to take it and how much additional joy I could have gotten—and given—from it. But now I'm thinking, is *failure* even the right word? It really isn't. It's regret. AND, it taught me some critical things I needed to know in THIS current season of my life.

Here's the thing. There was a LOT of life lived in that story I just shared. If any of us were to write down—physically write or type out—a story they believe led to a failure, I think you would see what I see. (Maybe you already do—high-five!).

How can I look back at that story of an ambitious, passionate little girl who went after something like her life depended on it and call it a failure? I LIVED in that story. It was full of moments where I won. It was full of moments where I laughed and smiled and made other people smile. That was a journey, my friends. I faced fear down, but yes, I also succumbed to it. I was human. But I got up on stages in my wheelchair where I *knew* people were judging me, and underestimating me, and at times, humoring me. I did it anyway. And then I loved surprising them by not sucking. I also LOVED so much getting to see the impact it had on people when I did it and did it well.

Did I have a recording contract? Nope. Did I have a primetime TV show or get thrown in the air by cowboys? Nuh-uh. I was a girl from Austin, TX who was *TRYING* to be successful doing something I loved. I hadn't captured the dream yet. Yet I lived *moments* while *trying* to achieve the dream that have become some I am most proud of. Did I fail because I didn't close the deal? Of course not. Even in a story where ultimately, you feel like you lost or that you failed (because my ultimate goal in ALL of this was to get a recording contract and make singing my profession, right?), there are *moments* of winning.

When I made the decision to walk away from music, even though my pride was hurt, and I hated having to look at the people I felt like I was partly trying to prove something to—that I COULD make it as a singer—and knowing that I hadn't made it and was going to continue working a traditional, "safe," corporate job, and feeling like maybe I wasn't as special as I had hoped I was, was it something I can call a failure? I think that would be a mistake.

It's just not as black and white as all that. Our self-worth is wrapped up so much in what we perceive as winning and losing, isn't it? If I look back at these experiences and THIS goal and all I see is the ultimate failure to secure a recording contract and elbow Trisha Yearwood down the charts (Trisha, call me and let's be besties together with Barbara Mandrell!), that isn't going to do anything good for my self-esteem, or my future ambition or ability to set and reach goals.

I'm not saying it's easy—none of this is easy. If it were, we wouldn't need books to help reframe our perspective. What I am saying is that it's worth it to get intentional about how you think about things and how you see your life's experiences.

The truth is, I was heartbroken. Making that call to the producer and quitting, I felt something die in me. Dramatic, but true. But also, I felt relief and I felt like a responsible grown-up taking charge of my education, my security, and my future. And that was exciting in its own new way. But, then, I felt sad and defeated and embarrassed. I felt guilty for letting my producer down. But I also realized there were NEW possibilities ahead of me.

Nope. It's not as simple as failing. I challenge any of you to write out a story you believe led to a failure. Write about the events that went into that experience. Write about the people who were along for the ride. Write about the people who watched. The steps you took—the places you went. Write about the moments you were SURE you were going to succeed, before something went south. Write about the decisions you made and the decisions that were made FOR YOU. It's complicated. And you didn't fail. You learned. You *lived*. You were redirected to a different place than you may have intended to go, but maybe you were led where you *needed* to go. Maybe that's clear now—maybe it's not, but it's where you went. Maybe you DID sabotage yourself. There are things to be learned from that, too.

In my own sabotage or quitting, I learned more about what I wanted in life. I learned about regret. I learned about perseverance, and I gained the drive NOT to quit on my next endeavor. I have spent ten years working on the dream to write this book, picking myself up after every rejection because I was determined not to quit again. Not to have to wonder "what if?"

I gained a 20-year career in high-tech where I learned about project management, and operations, and managing teams. I was challenged to grow in OTHER ways, and I gained skills that are helping me build this business as a speaker, writer, and podcast host. I built a retirement account. I met incredible people who inspired me and who became mentors and who set the bar high. I also met people I'd rather not meet again, but if I did, I know how to navigate them.

I think we get hung up on a wish. A wish that the goal had been conquered or that we'd achieved the thing that we were trying to achieve. We have regret and we have sadness and we have shame over the lack of achievement and THAT becomes a failure in our minds because we need to label it. Stop it.

You're doing yourself SUCH a disservice. There are moments in that story where YOU WON! Even if it wasn't the outcome you wanted, you were taught. You became stronger. You had impact. You may have learned to be gracious or perseverant or determined or creative. If your life or your profession or your relationship was redirected, how have you won at THAT as a result? Are there people who've come into your life who maybe wouldn't have if you'd "won" at the other thing? Maybe. And maybe they have changed everything for you, for the better. Maybe you've gone on to do and to be successful at other things it would never have occurred to you to dream of. Maybe because the other thing didn't pan out, maybe you got ONE moment along the way somewhere that was so worth it, but haven't given it the credit or acknowledgement it deserves. And maybe you feel like you've gone on to be ordinary. What if the other path had led to some other kind of destruction you never could have seen coming? Even ordinary beats destruction. We just don't know, so why beat ourselves up?

Looking back, and yes, hindsight is 20-20, I can see so much that I couldn't see in those disappointing moments when I didn't win the Grammy. When we are in a place where we feel like we are failing, it can be hard to see anything other than that. But when you can manage it, write that story out or play it out in your mind, or tell it to a friend over wine. Pick out the pieces where you WON. I promise you; they are there. They are the stories you'll tell your grandkids. Honor the moments where you won. THAT is how you turn a failure into a win.

As an aside, besides putting this to work in your own life, if you are a leader of any kind, if you can get comfortable with this idea, you're going to be a MUCH better leader for it. Who wouldn't want a boss or a parent who rather than placing blame and coming down on their team or their kids for "failing," can instead, encourage them to find the winning moments and learn and see how this outcome might have been a blessing in disguise?

I'm kind of having an "It's a Wonderful Life" moment (again) right now, but if I hadn't "failed" at music, my life could have looked SO much different, and who knows whether that would have been good or bad? I, personally, don't believe these things happen by accident. I believe there is something bigger than me guiding my path—I know I have free will, but I don't believe I am the only driver in my car.

If music had been successful for me, OR, if I'd opted not to go back to school and had a less ambitious career while pursuing music but never quite "made it," who knows how my life would be different. Maybe one of those paths would have meant I didn't become a mother. Maybe I wouldn't be writing this book right now. Maybe a music career would have been lonely and superficial and I could have missed out on the opportunity to do what I am doing today and speaking directly to people who need someone to show them what *their* potential is. Or maybe it would have been amazing and I could have impacted lives through music. Maybe I would have married Bradley Cooper and we'd be proud owners of a Pug Cafe and I'd have 16 Grammys and eight gold records lining the walls of my office.

Maybe. That's the thing about what ifs and maybes. No one knows. No one knows how much better or how much worse life would have been. All you can do is examine the story where you believe failure happened, and find your winning moments. Failure be danged!

Through that process, in addition to honoring where you've been and all you've done and the efforts you've made, you'll be able to see where you are now with a lot more clarity. Taking the word "failure" out of the equation gives you a different perspective on where you are now and on how meant-to-be your current place is. Maybe it can shine a new light on your purpose and on what is important and help guide your path forward.

Chapter 4:
Vanity

I have an awards event to attend on Wednesday, and I have nothing to wear. I promise you I am not being dramatic. I have *nothing* to wear. It's been a loooooooong time since I've needed to dress in cocktail attire. Did I say it's been a loooooooong time? It's actually been a loooooooooooooooong time. Coming off a year of COVID quarantine and then ten years before that when I had exactly zero fancy events to go to, I have NOTHING to wear.

I've been looking—mostly online, but nevertheless, I've been looking—for weeks! Nothing. It is now four days away, and yes. I am freaking out. I refuse to go to the event naked (you're welcome!), and I also refuse to NOT go to this super-cool event I am SO stoked to go to for the super-lame reason that I don't have anything to wear.

But seriously. I have nothing. And here is why I haven't been able to find anything. When you are five feet tall, and sit 100% of the time, AND have a physical disability that affects your physical form (short torso, no tone, some scoliosis leftover from childhood), you have a body that is really, really hard to find clothes for that flatter. Over the years, I've become an expert in dressing my body, and I have identified what does and doesn't work for me—the list of what DOES work is…shorter. Here is an illustration of what *some* of the "Dressing Mindy Rules" are. Just for the "dresses" category—never mind jeans, pants, shorts, tops…

- I can't wear what is a long dress for someone else because (number 1) I am five feet tall, and (number 2) I sit 100% of the time, which makes a long dress even longer. So, a long dress, is way too long. I know—I could have it shortened, but (number one) who has the time and money, and (number two) it's actually not always possible, because once you cut off the *amount* of length you'd have to cut off, sometimes the cut of the dress no longer works. Which leads me to my second requirement.

- Because I have to get the dress on my body while in a seated position, down around and under the "hip and thigh area," (can only lean side to side and forward to get it tucked, I don't have the arm-strength to push myself up to yank said dress under) it can't be a straight cut—a "swing" or "trapeze" style cut is the most ideal—nope, not even an A-line cut. Not full enough.

- Again, because I have to get the dress on a body in a seated position, down around and under the "hip and thigh area," the fabric needs to have stretch. So, I'm talking, like a knit or a sweater dress (which I recognize is not cocktail material) is what I have to stick to. Cotton, linen, denim—any fabric with no "give" is too rigid to get under and around me, tucked and smoothed and looking right. Fabric with some "give" also just lays in a much more flattering way.

- No spaghetti straps, no strapless, no off-the-shoulder, no one-shoulder, no styles that cut way in on the shoulder/neck area like is so trendy right now, etc. Now things are getting personal, but I vowed to be honest. I can't do a strapless bra because of my posture situation, so anything without a sleeve of some sort is out because otherwise, I have bra-strap issues.

- I'm also picky about necklines—okay, this falls more into the *preference* category, but I have a very short neck, so a V-neck or a scoop neck is the most flattering and what I tend to look for.

Hopefully you can see in my list above, how very limited I am in terms of what I have to choose from, and why—after weeks of trying—I still have nothing to wear to this event. I know we ALL have preferences about what looks good on us and maybe a few limitations due to body shape, etc., but as a very short, disabled, non-ambulatory woman, my fashion options are WAY limited. And vanity is a royal pain in my side.

See, I am a girly-girl. No doubt about it. I love clothes, shoes, makeup, and a good lash extension. I love when my hair is having a good day. I love highlights and the perfect haircut. SNS nails changed my life. I *love* being a girly-girl. It's fun. The limitations I have around living up to it, however, suck.

This is not a new topic of conversation. As long as I have been alive (I see you, daughter—stifle the "age jokes"), this has been a struggle for women all over the world. If you turn on the television or open a magazine, you can't help but be bombarded with EXCESSIVE ads and articles and makeover shows about how we should all look younger, and better. I have DEFINITELY spent way too much time in my life believing them. I've spent a lot of time hating the reflection in the mirror (or avoiding mirrors altogether) because I didn't want to face what I would certainly see—someone who wasn't good enough.

Every stinking day, I saw the models and the pop stars and the movie stars and the ads and all these things that desensitize us to what the idea of normal is. It's not even a conscious choice. Because the images become ingrained in daily life, those images in our minds become the ones to define "normal" and what we are supposed to live up to. Guess what I NEVER saw in an ad, or a movie, or on a stage of any kind? A woman in a wheelchair. My 18-year-old self somewhere along the way decided that was because a woman in a wheelchair wasn't okay. Wasn't what the world wanted to see, or to love, or to model.

All I know is that, every time I looked in the mirror, I failed to see what was expected. What was normal. What was acceptable. And seeing something I thought was SO FAR from it, was gut-wrenching. I spent every day of my life unable to do what other people could do, and facing limitations. When the limitations showed up in the mirror, too, it was like the straw that broke the camel's back. It made me hate myself. Completely superficial, of course, but it was real for me and for my sense of confidence.

Like I said before, when you have a disability that affects your physical form, achieving that norm of perfection becomes that much less realistic.

I grew up with a weight problem. I was always a little heavy, and I also saw my lack of muscle tone as fat. Because of my disability, the entire category of exercise was taken off the table—aerobics, running, walking, lifting, tennis, kickboxing, yoga, dancing, and swimming. None of that was in my personal bag of tricks for tools to stay healthy and fit ("healthy and fit" are my choice of words today. Back then, the word I would have chosen was "thin." It was ALL ABOUT being thin and pretty). Everything *I thought* I had available to me to stay healthy and to look the way I wanted to look was in the kitchen. It became about deprivation. And deprivation leads to resentment. And resentment leads to spiteful activity (i.e., eating everything you can get your hands on to show "them," whoever *that* is). Spiteful activity leads to guilt and shame, which leads back to deprivation, where the whole cycle begins again.

When I was in my twenties, I was stuck in this cycle for years and resorted to behaviors the cycle accommodated to try to help me achieve the vision of what I thought I was supposed to be. I would live on Diet Coke for three days. Then I would binge. Sometimes, I binged and purged. I *wrecked* my body—this body that was ALREADY weakened and fragile. I see now that I should have been *cherishing* this body and *nurturing* it. When someone is fragile and weakened—is further abuse what they need? Of course not, but that is what I gave myself.

I can remember, one night I was at a breaking point. I had made myself so sick. Going from one extreme to the other is not good for your body, in case you were wondering. And I was paying the price. I was having awful intestinal issues and couldn't figure out how to re-regulate things. I was sick, and I was in pain. I was hungry, but I was terrified of food. I was so exhausted. I was just sobbing. I was scared.

Here is the kicker. I was doing all these things to myself to try to look a certain way, but it wasn't working!! I was still overweight. I STILL didn't look the way I wanted to look. AND, I felt awful. Talk about frustration of the highest order. Thoughts of, "Why can't I just get this right?" dominated.

The next day was the day I got it right. I made an appointment with a therapist. I was FINALLY at a point where I could see how flawed what I was doing was. I knew this was not how I was supposed to feel. I knew it wasn't even getting me any closer to what I ultimately wanted—to look good. Even then, though, I couldn't see that *the goal* I had was flawed. I wanted to look good. What I should have wanted for myself was to feel good and to be healthy. PS—feeling good and being healthy typically leads to looking good. I couldn't see it, though. I knew what I was doing was all wrong, and I also knew I couldn't fix it by myself. This was years of programming that had to be undone. THAT was the real problem—my thinking. No can of Diet Coke or binge-fest was going to cure my thinking.

Guess what happened? I got healthy. I think I was about 24 years old, and as my therapist and I started peeling back the layers, I began making good choices in the kitchen. I started eating protein and vegetables. I started to *want* to nourish myself. I accepted the fact that there was not an unlimited amount of carbs my sedentary body could actually use before it would store them. And I began to realize, that fact didn't make me a bad person or a lesser person than anyone else. It was just a fact of my physical make up. It didn't happen overnight—don't get me wrong. This was a process. Even once I started losing weight, it took me a long time to start buying clothes that fit my smaller body because of the body dysmorphia and my brain still thought I was thirty pounds overweight when I looked in the mirror. But eventually, I got there and when I was 25 or 26, I finally truly felt pretty for the first time ever in my life—ever.

We'll talk about dating in another chapter because, news flash! Dating sucks—it can also be awesome, but I digress. The point I want to make is that—the guys started to notice. I was getting attention and going on dates for the first time in my adult life. I had confidence. I had energy and I was finally healthy—body *and* mind.

I wish I could say that was the end of the story, folks. This has been a lifelong struggle, and there have been triggers in life that have caused me to regress. I put a lot of weight back on after I got married and struggled to take it off for years. I am that mom whose daughter will have very few pictures of her mother growing up because I avoided the camera.

Last year, though, I got a health coach after trying all the fad diets and things that don't work, and again, I was reminded that it was all in my mind. If my story sounds at all familiar to you—I am not a therapist or a nutritionist—but take it from me, how we feel, how we look and our journey to become healthy, confident people begins in our minds. The only thing that has EVER worked for me was to have someone who was qualified help me understand my thoughts, my behaviors, my habits, and my programming. You can eat all the celery you want, but I truly believe—based on experience—you must get your mind right if you want to get your body right.

Here is another thing I've learned. We ALL have an optimal level of health we can achieve. And I'm not talking about becoming a body-builder. Despite my illness and my physical limitations, I DO HAVE an *optimal* level of heath I can achieve for MY body. It looks nothing like a body builder or an Iron Man, but it is unique to me—my weight, my blood pressure, my cholesterol, my blood sugar, my stress levels. There are things within my power to work on, in a healthy way, that will affect every single one of those things. Being at my best possible level of health will, by extension, cause me to feel my best possible level of energy and joy and confidence. Also, though—my optimal level of health will not look like yours, or hers, or theirs, and vice versa. You can't compare—you see the trouble that got me in to. Notice, I am not saying "perfect" level of health—I am saying "optimal." Perfection is a myth and is the thing that sets our path down these destructive roads. If anyone tries to tell you otherwise, they are a filthy liar.

At various points in my life, I made a lot of excuses (I still do every once in a while; I'm human). I made excuses about how I couldn't be healthy or thin or fit because I couldn't exercise. I made excuses that I couldn't be healthy because I didn't have time to cook healthy foods, and I HAD to get the burger and fries because that was just all I had time for. I made excuses about my genetics and my metabolism. I made excuse after excuse.

But what are excuses, anyway? Excuses are lies we tell ourselves so we won't have to do the hard work we don't want to do. And any journey to health is hard—I have tried every shortcut known to man. Save yourself the heartache. Learn from me in minutes what I took a lifetime to learn. Shortcuts don't work. The end. THAT is another truth that sucks. You HAVE to make hard, un-fun choices and do things you'd rather not do and invest time you'd rather spend doing other things if you are on a quest to get healthy. Think about it like this, changing your health means changing your cellular makeup in your body—fat cells, muscle mass, chemistry—there is no overnight way to make that happen, AND when I, personally, think about it that way—it's so cool! Our bodies and what they can do is fascinating.

Excuses will only delay your progress. I had to stop lying to myself because I didn't like the reality of my health, and I wanted something different. I know I'm being blunt and harsh, but it's only because I feel so passionately. I've said a lot about the journey being hard, and it is. But guys, when you accomplish your goals, and you feel good, and your numbers in the doctor's office change, and you have energy and you gain confidence, and you know that YOU did that?? NOTHING feels better. You may have to make 100 smaller hard choices and do 100 smaller hard things to get there, but DANG!! Does it ever feel good! Anyone, in my book, who hits *any* health goal in a healthy way genuinely earns "badass" status, because it's haaaaaard. Do it anyway. My health coach said something so simple to me that has become a mantra in my life— "the common denominator between every single person who has ever achieved a goal is that they didn't quit." I wrote my master's degree thesis in accountability (true story!). I don't like excuses.

THESE ARE THE THINGS magazines and TV ads should show daily as beautiful. People who are making good choices, doing the hard work and who are as healthy as THEY can be—short, tall, black, white, standing or sitting in a wheelchair.

Let's tie this up in a bow. We—especially women—are SO hard on ourselves. My story is one small example of how hard we are on ourselves, and the damage we do to ourselves by having unhealthy standards, role models, and practices to try to attain what we think the world says we should be.

There is only one me. There is only one you. That is special and it should be honored. We all deserve to be cherished and nurtured and treated well, regardless of what anyone else might be telling you—explicitly OR implicitly—with the images imposed on us daily.

My wish is this—beauty brands, Hollywood, Nashville, Broadway— show the little girls of this world that ALL women are beautiful—black, white, Latina, Asian, physically disabled, developmentally disabled—we ALL exist. We are ALL special, and we ALL deserve to see that the world sees us, accepts us, and maybe even wants to model us and celebrate us as an everyday part of this society. We are women who do amazing things and present beauty in our own, individual ways. Give us a voice. Let the little girls of the world see that it is okay, and maybe even exceptional, to be who they are, regardless of size, color, or physical ability.

Chapter 5:
Loneliness

How many country songs have been written about loneliness? Spoiler alert: a lot. That's because loneliness is such a big part of the human condition. It's something we all feel. It's something we all want to solve for. It's something we can ALL relate to. I truly don't think I could find anyone on the planet who hasn't felt lonely ever in their life. And, when we do, it sucks. I could write an entire book about all the times I've felt loneliness in my life, but for the purpose of THIS book, I'll keep it to a chapter.

The first time I remember truly being lonely was in middle school. In fact, "Middle School" should probably be a chapter in this book because middle school sucks. Now, if you have a child in middle school, I'm sure they are the exception and they are a delight, but also if you have a child in middle school, surely, you know from experiencing the kids they see every day, middle school kids are the worst.

It's such a hard age from 11 to 13 or 14, your social life is changing, boys and girls are noticing each other and dating. Cliques form—there are cool kids, athletes, bookworms. Hormones are raging. Relationships are changing. Competition is emerging. Suddenly, there is drama galore, and one day you can be the most popular kid in school. The next, you're a pariah. My heart is beating a little faster and harder just thinking about being back there.

In middle school, I was part of a group of kids who weren't the ultra-coolest, but we were pretty darn cool. We loved a good sleepover. We watched movies. We painted our nails and experimented with lip gloss (scandalous!). We consumed "Teen" magazine like it was going out of style and were beginning to pay attention to who the emerging heart-throbs in Hollywood were. We had secret crushes that only our best friend knew about (who am I kidding—probably the whole school knew. We were not masters of subtlety yet).

I went to middle school in a tiny town in Florida that had one stoplight. The middle school had three options for electives you could take, so most kids took them all. And then, we took them again—Home Economics, Typing (okay, this was 1980-something) and Industrial Arts.

I was in eighth grade, and I'd already taken Home Ec. and Typing—twice, I think. Industrial Arts was kind of like woodshop, but maybe a little fancier. As the girly-girl I've already claimed to be, I put off Industrial Arts as looooong as I could, but it was time to broaden my horizons, so I signed up. Turns out, there was a girl in that class who HATED me. No really, HATED. I don't know why—she was a "tough-guy" type, and I was a little shy and mousey—maybe she thought I was a goody-goody (and I probably was), but she had it out for me. I'd go into class and deal with smart comments and snide remarks, and then once, she snuck up behind me and CUT MY HAIR! No joke—she snuck up from behind and I felt a little something on the back of my head and then I heard it… snip. She walked away from me, holding up the CHUNK of hair and smiling. Psychopath.

During this time, I was also on "the outs" with my peer group. I'd had a series of fights with my best friend, and we were in a "not speaking" phase and the other members of our social group had sided with her. I went to school, and no one much spoke to me. The phone stopped ringing, and I didn't dare call anyone. There were no sleepover invitations. I was alone a lot, and I was so sad. Looking back, I can see that I was a little temperamental and had *of course* played a role in the "break-up" with my best friend, for sure, but back then, when I was 13, I had been *so wronged*. But, regardless of who did what to who, I was completely alienated, I was being bullied, and it led to a scary time for me.

I was already a 13-year-old girl, dealing with the emotional baggage of being in a wheelchair—at the age when the worst thing that can happen to you is to be different than everyone else, I WAS different than everyone else. And if that weren't bad enough, I was being bullied and had been wholly rejected by my social group.

Obviously, this was before life had fully unfolded (shoot—at 47 it's STILL unfolding. Can I get an "Amen?") and all I had were limited experiences to compare to and reaction-based responses to other 13-year-old, immature indictments and rejections. My self-esteem tanked and most of my moments were filled with negative thoughts that became my truth—the only things I *could* believe. So much so, I wanted to die when I was 13.

Thirteen. And I wanted to die. For a period, (unbeknownst to them) if my parents left the house, I was afraid of what I would do to myself. I went through a time period so traumatic where despite the supportive family I had that taught me I was worthy, and despite the opportunities I had to serve as the Texas AND Florida state poster child for the Muscular Dystrophy Association where I got to do cool things like be on TV and give speeches, I still had all of the insecurities and the self-hatred of my disability and of how different I was. I believed that I was unworthy of anyone's time or friendship, AND, during this time in my life, being rejected by my social circle, and being bullied at school only further perpetuated my belief that there was nothing redeemable in me. I didn't believe there was anything to look forward to. That is precisely where my loneliness led me on this leg of my journey.

Now, you know me, I'm all about finding purpose. Let's talk about "why" for a second. Why on Earth would a 13-year-old girl have to go through bullying, a crippling disability, and self-esteem issues so bad that she is suicidal?

So that I could find out how brave, how strong, how beautiful, how smart, how resilient I was. That's why. Do you know how I figured that out? One day my mom told me about affirmations and looking in the mirror and telling myself I was pretty. And (begrudgingly, at first) I did it. And over time, it worked.

When I was only 13, I came to see that our thoughts and what we tell ourselves very directly correspond to the way we feel about ourselves. I realized there was something more there than the desperation and the loneliness I was feeling, and I started to look for it. I worked HARD to find the answer. I also heard a statement one day that left a big impression on my 13-year-old mind—"suicide is a permanent solution to a temporary problem." Those words blew my barely teenaged mind.

I was 13 and never could have articulated this, but what I somehow knew was that I wanted there to be more to that suffering than JUST the suffering. I wanted there to be a reason and a purpose, so I opened my mind and my heart, and I set out to find one. Or two, or three. And not only did I find purpose behind it, but because I *owned* the mission to find the purpose, it was purpose that made me a better person. When I was 13. Even then, I was an emerging badass.

In fact, I credit some of my worst days with so many of my best qualities—qualities that my struggles instilled in me—strength, courage, determination, ambition, perseverance, creativity, being comfortable in my own skin and cultivating a sense of humor. By the way, these are the same qualities I needed to employ in my life to accomplish almost every goal I've ever attempted. Hmmm…

As hard as it was, I kept showing up. I went to school every day. I faced the bully (my mom had reported her to the principal for cutting my hair and she started to back off). I faced the peer group who wanted nothing to do with me. I went home and spent time alone, and learned that was okay, and learned to appreciate my own company. Most importantly, though, I survived the loneliness, and I am still here.

It must be said that bullying *these days* with the online world I didn't have to deal with back then, comes with lots of new ways to manifest. Any bullying is beyond NOT okay, and should be taken seriously. Bullying also is not reserved for teenagers. I read Jamie Kern Lima's awesome book *Believe It* recently where she talked about being bullied by grown women who were business competitors. It happens to lots of us. And, I'll say it again. It's not okay, however and whenever it shows up. It should be taken seriously.

Now, not all bouts of loneliness need be as dramatic as this. This is probably the example from my life where the *consequences* of my loneliness were the most severe, but in looking back, I can say that experiencing this loneliness and the fallout of the loneliness and being forced to find my resilience set me up well for future loneliness. And oh, sweet Jesus, yes—there has been so much more.

When I was 16, for example. What is the big event that most teenagers celebrate when they are 16? Driving! Except, my disability prevented me from being able to drive back then, and I couldn't get into my friend's cars.

I should say here—we moved away from Florida the summer after 8th grade. My dad was transferred to be the administrator of a hospital in Austin, TX, and THAT, my friends was a godsend for me. There was no sign of being reabsorbed into my friend circle, and I was thrilled to have the chance to go somewhere new and start over. And yes, I made new friends.

So, back to age 16. My parents had a super-cool full-sized Ford Econoline van with a wheelchair lift built into it. That was the only such vehicle at the time that could be outfitted for a wheelchair ramp. My friends (for the most part) were not allowed to drive it, and the kiss of death when you are 16 is to have you mom or dad pull up in the old Ford Econoline to drop you off at a party. So again, I stayed home most Friday and Saturday nights, learning to be happy spending time…with me.

This was also the year when friends started strutting their new driver's licenses to go off campus for lunch during the week. I couldn't even think about sitting alone in the cafeteria, so most days, I took my lunch to the choir room (where I don't want to brag, but I was kind of a big fish—VP of the honors choir. Try not to be jealous!) and ate by myself there, where no one could judge me.

Loneliness has followed me for so much of my life. Dating? Not so much until I was in my mid-late twenties. I found high school and college boys…and young adult men…not to be terribly interested in dating the girl in the wheelchair. Lonely.

I've had almost every one of my best adult friends move away. My absolute best friend on the planet moved to New Zealand, for crying out loud (love you, Eileen!). Turns out, adults have families and jobs and other circumstances that require them to move to different cities or states or countries, thus, leaving friends behind.

So often, I have found myself in situation after situation where I have been lonely. I know that there are probably a lot of other circumstances YOU may have found yourself in. Romantic break-ups and divorce. Death of a spouse or of anyone you're close to, for that matter. Moving to a new city where you don't know anyone. Starting a new job where you are the outsider. So many ways we can find ourselves alone.

What's the actual problem with loneliness, though? It calls into question one of a human's most basic needs: connection. In fact, it is the third most foundational need of humans according to Maslow's hierarchy of needs (after our basic needs such as food and water, and our need for safety and security).

When we are lonely, it's usually, of course, because of some real or perceived absence of other people. We either have been isolated, or have maybe isolated ourselves. I will also say—and I continue to maintain, I am not a therapist (although, I'm beginning to think I *should have been...*)—I think it's even possible to feel lonely while you're standing in a crowded room full of people as a result of our emotional states. We could go super deep here, but I will leave it to the *actual* professionals.

So, what do we do, then? First and foremost, there are definite times when I would say to seek help. Talk to a counselor or therapist. It's hard to note every possible scenario of loneliness, but when things turn to a heavy emotional level—you feel hopeless or, heaven forbid, suicidal, I'll be the first one to say, find a counselor and go do the work to feel better and to ensure your own health and safety.

I know it can feel like you've failed—you haven't. The strength is in standing up and making (and going to) that appointment. Admitting you may have more happening than you can deal with on your own, takes courage, my friend. I would even venture to say that *nowadays,* there are more people who see a therapist than who don't. Therapy has become so standard and so accepted. It is not something anyone should feel ashamed for having done or for needing to do.

Second? Enjoy the solitude. I know that may sound weird, but life is crazy so much of the time, yes? We have jobs and responsibilities. If you find yourself in a space where you are lonely because you started a new job, a friend moved away, you moved to a new city…take a minute and enjoy. Because, guess what? Your current state won't be that way much longer.

Take the time to immerse yourself in the job or the city and figure it aaaaaall out. Explore. Do the things YOU want to do the way YOU want to do them while you still can. You can learn a lot about yourself, as I've seen, when you spend time with yourself. You can listen to your thoughts. You can journal. You can reconnect with what's important to you and why. You can figure out what's really cool about you and put more of that out there into the world. You can take the time to learn a new subject or hobby, which can lead to meeting people!

As I've said before, sometimes it's okay to not be okay for a minute. If you are sitting in loneliness, feel it. Think about it. Reflect on why you are here, where you've been and where you want to go. Let it be. There is a lot to be said for acceptance of your current state and letting it play out.

I think that one big problem with loneliness, though, in my experience, is that it can wreak a bit of havoc with our self-esteem. If you're lonely or isolated for too long or too many times, like my 13-year-old self, you can begin to question whether there is something wrong with you or why you're not wanted, not sought after, not needed. Again, sometimes, these are thoughts that require a therapist to break us free from. But I think there are some very constructive ways to address them on your own as well, or in addition to seeking therapy.

Take the opportunity to do a self-inventory. Who are you? What do you value? What are your good qualities? What are the qualities you'd like to change? What are the qualities you'd like to acquire? Guess what? We are always changing—sometimes naturally, and sometimes we change by choice. If you want more of one thing and less of another thing, be intentional and focus on it. YOU are in control.

Know this. We ALL get lonely. Just that alone makes you a member of a club. It doesn't mean there is something wrong with you. It means that this is a season, perhaps, where you are meant to learn, or to make room in your life and your heart for new people. Again, I will bring up the self-fulfilling prophecy. If you can find a way to let this be a constructive, productive blip on the radar and open yourself to new things and people—I 100% believe that is what you'll get.

Find the purpose in the loneliness. Like me, is it going to cultivate strength and courage in you? Is it going to give you a minute to breathe and to be selfish (in a good way)? Is it because you are meant to make space for new people in your life? Is it because you are meant to let someone go? I will quote Oprah all day long and twice on Tuesday, "Sometimes the universe whispers, sometimes it shouts." Is this a whisper you should listen closer to? Or is it a shout because you missed the other signs?

Hear this. There is nothing wrong with you. You are here, walking this Earth for a reason. It is not a mistake. SO, get to know YOU. Learn to appreciate YOU. Discover why you're so awesome to spend time with. Find joy. Joy is contagious and will attract others to you, so grab all you can! And again, look for the lessons this time is teaching you and take them to heart. I guarantee it can make you a better human in some way.

Chapter 6:
Overwhelm

My first thought after the car crash was, "My car. The car that takes a year to build. The car that costs $130,000, that was ALMOST paid off, and that I don't have the money to replace. Oh my god. She's destroyed my life for the next year and a half. I won't leave my house for a year." There may-or-may-not have been several expletives interspersed amongst these thoughts.

We sat, our cars nose-to-nose. Her head was laying on her inflated air-bag, and she meekly raised it to look at me. I glared daggers at her through the windshield. The impact had flung me like a sack of potatoes over the arm of my wheelchair, my atrophied muscles unable to lift my trunk back to a sitting position, my neck barely strong enough to raise my head up to look at her. Then, expressionless, she put her head back down on the airbag and I thought, "Oh my gosh, is she okay??" As witnesses shouted at me through the driver's window, I just started to cry.

I'd just had my annual checkup with my doctor and was headed back to work, when, stopped at a red light on highway 360, I saw a white SUV turn left into my lane from a parking lot on the right side of the street and start driving toward me, gaining speed. My calm, rational self-thought, "Ok, she's going to figure out she turned the wrong way and stop in a second." Just in case, though, I looked left to the drop-off beside me, and then to the line of cars standing still to my right. Huh. Nowhere to go, I realized. And yep, she was still coming, I also realized. For reasons I still can't explain today (except that upon those two realizations, I froze) it didn't occur to me to blast my horn at her. Finally, right before the impact, I thought, "this is going to hurt."

In a situation like this, for me (of course, for everyone, but maybe to a greater extent because of my mobility challenges, for me), things become complicated really quickly, and overwhelm is plentiful. My car was a goner. I wasn't going to be driving away from this mess. I was injured—the pain screaming in my ankles and right wrist made that clear. I didn't think anything was broken, but I knew I wasn't fine. The paramedic had checked me out and was coming back from the ambulance with a bandage to wrap my wrist shaking his head. Apparently, by then, the other driver was curled into a fetal position on a stretcher, speaking gibberish. She was so high on who knows what.

Destination one—the emergency room. Except, if the ambulance took me, I'd have to be separated from my 300-pound motorized wheelchair, which is essentially my surrogate legs. You couldn't get this H-E-A-V-Y, non-folding wheelchair into any other car, so the police (bless their souls—they were SO kind to me) and I began problem-solving (which, by the way, is NOT what I wanted to be doing right then—problem-solving.) I was, you guessed it, instantly overwhelmed and I felt—physically—the weight of the immediate problems to solve. What I WANTED was to get taken care of, get my car towed and get to the emergency room. But what other choice was there? No one else was familiar with the unique limitations of my situation or how to help me. I spoke with several police officers, explaining how this needed to go.

Action was all that was going to get me anywhere and police began getting on the phone to dispatchers trying to figure out how to get me AND my wheelchair a ride to the ER. There were wheelchair accessible cabs in Austin, but dispatch told us they were all in use and it would be 90 minutes before one could get to us. It occurred to me that the adaptive car place that had built my car was about 45 minutes north of us with accessible rentals and I knew their staff well. Police called them and asked if a good Samaritan there could come drive me. To which they, of course, said yes and began making their way to me.

Seriously—I must stop a second and just comment on the kindness and compassion SO MANY humans show when they see someone in distress. ALREADY, a bad situation was made so much better as I finally smiled and laughed through tears as the police updated me and joked to make me smile.

Then, an accessible cab pulled up at the scene to take me to the ER—they'd pulled a rabbit out of a hat, somehow, and I was on my way.

I got home from the ER, finally, around 11 pm that night—mind you, the accident happened around 12:30 pm. See, I'm also complicated in a hospital. I had bruising from the seatbelt across my abdomen and chest so bad, the ER doctor had *thought* I had internal bleeding, and I needed an MRI or a CAT scan. But I can't stand, and I can't "just" be lifted. A patient lift (the single ONE the hospital had) had to be located and brought to us to get me into the "scanners." Then the imaging staff—who doesn't normally have this complication or the extra, unfamiliar equipment—they had to figure out how to use the patient lift and move me into the "scanner." For the same reasons, I am tricky to X-ray, and I had multiple parts and pieces still screaming at me that needed to be X-rayed. Then, you wait for results, then you go back for more X-rays when the view wasn't good enough, then you wait for the doctor to see you, then you wait for prescriptions, then you wait for discharge papers—THEN, we went through the whole process to get another one of those rare accessible cabs to come pick us up. Ugh. Exhausted, and finally diagnosed with two sprained ankles and a sprained right wrist and all the bruising, I finally made it home and got to sleep.

In the morning, I awoke to the new reality of my life. No car, no way to get to work. No way to get anywhere. I opted to baby myself and me and my injured parts stayed in bed that next day, but I knew I didn't have the luxury of lazing-about. I felt the urgency of my employment situation and of keeping my employment situation—new $130,000 car now needed—so I got to work making a plan.

- Call my boss
- Call the insurance company and get a claim filed
- Call the place that built my car and find out how to quickly get through the insurance and financing rigamarole and begin the process to get a new car
- Call a lawyer—I am not a litigious person, but this was going to be too complicated and too expensive a case to just let the insurance companies sort through

My husband and I spent so much time on the phone that day. I was hurting—physically AND emotionally. I'd been stripped of my independence. Just because a 19-year-old girl had decided to get high at noon on a Wednesday afternoon and then get behind the wheel of a car. I was angry. And I was so sad and frustrated, knowing what lay ahead for the next year. Me, pretty much on house-arrest.

The good news? By the end of the day, I had some of a plan. I had a start toward repairing the situation and I had the right people informed and on-board to help. Then, I got to watch trash TV for the rest of the night and rest, feeling sad, angry and frustrated, but in-control.

If you are in the midst of some kind of overwhelm right now, I have good news. You've already taken AT LEAST a first step. The first step is the hardest. It may be scary. Unknowns are scary, and you may not know the right course of action yet. You may be afraid to take a wrong step. Please, try to let yourself realize that ANY step is a right step. Reading this book—looking for motivation or ideas—is a step. Research shows that before a person can take action or feel ready to take action, they need to first believe that their situation or circumstances CAN improve or change. And if you are reading this book, I BELIEVE that you either DO believe change is possible, OR you WANT TO believe it's possible. Let me be clear right. This. Second. Whatever "it" is—it *can* get better. You may have to help it get there, but it *CAN*.

Guess what else—working through your emotions and belief system around your circumstances, ALSO ACTION. Which means you've potentially taken not just one, but TWO STEPS in the direction of healing. See? I've got you, Boo!

There are things that I've learned to implement when I am overwhelmed that change the game. But it's not just me—so many of the things I've learned to do are the very same things people I've interviewed, studied, or spoken to also do. One of them is to let people help you.

Seriously, this is SO hard for me, I can't even. As a type-A, slightly OCD (self-diagnosed), control-freak, this is one of the hardest things I've EVER learned to do. Did I mention that I am FIERCELY independent? Those qualities in me, combined with THIS disabled person's mindset around not wanting to be a burden or to appear as incapable, make it SO HARD for me to accept help. ESPECIALLY if it's something I know I can do. I may have 9,000 other things vying for my attention, I may be in bed, physically injured or sick, but if it's something I KNOW is within my span of control and, however difficult or time-consuming, that I can do, it's SO hard for me to let someone else take the wheel. Even Jesus—amiright, Carrie Underwood??

I used to think it would make me look weaker if I accepted the help. And heaven forbid, I should inconvenience another human being as I lay in bed with two broken femurs like in the previous car accident.

Yup. Remember that OTHER car accident I mentioned a chapter or two ago? I broke both my femurs, and my right wrist and spent nearly two and a half months in the hospital. Did I let anyone bring us dinners after I got home (with two still very broken legs after I strong-armed the doctor into letting me go home sooner than I should have, because I'm a slightly OCD control-freak)? Are you kidding me? I even told my parents to stop visiting every day after a while because I felt I was inconveniencing them. Guess what happened then? We didn't get any help. And it was hard.

But then do you know what happened a few years later? My dad ended up in the hospital having surgery. I took meals to my parents. And I brought groceries over to their house. I did it without asking because as it turns out, the slightly OCD, control-freak gene runs in my family and when I offered to do these things for them, they told me, "No." But then I saw the relief and the gratitude on both their faces after I did it anyway, without their permission…and I felt SO good. AND I could see that it really had helped my mom.

I learned it really was a gift we could BOTH receive—the giver and the receiver. Have you ever done something nice for someone else in a time of need? Did it feel good? ABSOLUTELY. Remember that and decide to give someone else that feeling when you are overwhelmed.

There was another time a few years after the deer incident when I fell off a curb, catapulted my body out of my wheelchair and onto a parking garage floor, breaking my right arm right below the shoulder and right above my elbow (I know—I should just wrap myself in bubble-wrap!). More to come on this story later in the book.

This time, I only spent a week in the hospital, and when I got home, I had offers from coworkers and our church to bring meals to us. My autopilot started to say no, when the first offer from our church rolled in. And then, I stopped myself. I remember clearly, the fatigue and the pain and the overwhelm, and I remember this little voice in my mind that whispered, "what if you said 'yes' this time?" I stopped mid-sentence on the phone and I said, "You know what, that would actually be really helpful—yes, that would be great."

Guess what happened then. WE GOT HELP. And it was a miracle each time a meal showed up that we didn't have to cook. And what also happened was, no one thought I was incapable for accepting graciously offered meals while I had a severely broken arm, had just spent a week in the hospital, and had a daughter, a husband, two dogs, a cat and a house to take care of. Not one single person thought I was selfish, inept, or taking advantage. They were just. happy. to. help.

I know sometimes a problem is embarrassing or feels like something we want to keep private. But you'd be surprised if you heard some of what those very people you might be thinking about asking for help have gone through in their personal lives. We work so hard to keep things private, but honestly, there is so much power in sharing your story. It's exactly why

I'm writing this book. Because if we all knew how very NOT ALONE we are in what we're going through, we'd be amazed. So many of the women I've mentioned in these pages kept their adversity a secret. And those who did, told me the second they began sharing their struggles with people they trusted, they felt liberated and lighter. AND, they got help.

Know what else turned out to work in my favor when I'm overwhelmed and struggling? Being intentional and kind to myself. Wait, what? Who has time for that?? I do, and you do, if you want to get through it without turning into a complete looney-toon.

Remember Madison? She is my friend whose house flooded in Hurricane Harvey, then her father-in-law lost his battle with colon cancer, then her mother fought breast cancer, Madison totaled her car and then her dad texted her that he was divorcing her mother. Their first year and a half of marriage, and life hit them with everything it had. Sometimes, we receive more than our fair share of challenges.

When I spoke to her about her struggles, I asked her how she got through that time. She had a lot to say and it wasn't just one thing that got her through it. She said that initially, she felt overwhelmed and couldn't make sense of what was happening. She felt herself in a reactive mindset and was just barely treading water.

About midway through, however, she told me that something shifted, and she learned to be more intentional and began to move out of the emotional, reactive place she'd been residing in. When I asked her what she thought triggered that shift, she said that she realized that if she stayed in that reactive place, her relationships were going to suffer. Her relationships with her mom, with Alex, with friends—they held deep meaning in her life and became motivation to make a change and to begin to approach things more intentionally.

As part of this intentionality, Madison learned that you have to be kind to yourself too. She was trying to please everyone else and keep all those who were watching her suffer happy (can anyone relate??) and believing that everything would be okay, but she was neglecting herself.

Madison said, "Take things one day at a time. Slow down and have grace. Be with the people you love. Allow every day to be its own thing, and know that it's okay that the laundry's not done or that you dropped the ball at work. Make time a priority. Even hard time you won't get back. Prioritize what matters." Did I mention she is smart?

I know that initially, when tragedy strikes or something bad happens, it can be hard to be intentional. When you're overwhelmed, you're feeling all these knee-jerk negative emotions and it can be hard to even be intentional enough to put one foot in front of the other. Try. At some point, try.

Think about today—one thing, one minute, one day at a time, just like Madison says. And with every minute, day and thing, try to stop and make an active decision about how you want to handle it, who you want to show up as, and then decide what the right next thing is after that. Feeling and dealing with your emotions is important, but after a while, you must take the control back and not let the emotions rule the entirety of your existence.

The natural tendency of some of those reactive, negative responses will likely be negative self-talk and the tendency to be hard on yourself. Stop. What good does that do? Does it make the situation better or resolve faster? I don't think it does. So, be kind to others, be kind to yourself, don't sweat the small stuff (no one will know if you're rocking those jeans for the fourth day), and live with intention. YOU are in charge.

What I've learned is, once you are in a place where you're able to move from "reaction mode" to "intentional mode," that is when things start to get good. That is when you can plan and start to get on with it— whatever "it" looks like. And once you begin to take action, you build momentum, and that momentum becomes a renewable source of hope. You'll see progress being made, however slow (and if it's slow, DON'T give up). Any progress and control you can find will allow you to begin seeing glimmers of light at the end of the tunnel.

One thing I want to say about a plan up front, though, is, plans may change. And that's okay. It's important to realize that even though you're being intentional and practical and putting a plan in place, circumstances change, and details can change without our permission. Don't let that re-victimize you. I've heard too many people say too many times, "well, OF COURSE that didn't work. Of course, it all went wrong again. Of course, that would happen to me. I give up." I will hunt you down and I will find you—I promise. Do not let me hear you give up. You're better than that. You AND the people who love you deserve better than that.

Sometimes those deviations in your plans lead to better destinations than you'd imagined. Sometimes the new destination IS what you believed would be less ideal—try to just look at it as "different" instead of worse. Not worse—different. Our words have power. Keep an open mind and know that, to an extent, things will work out the way they are supposed to, and that no matter what, the time is going to pass and you're GOING TO get through it. If one thing doesn't work, try something else. I use the mantra, "I am a river. I bend, I flow" when the very solid plan I've created needs to deviate.

Having a plan is one of the things that Pamela—who I mentioned in a previous chapter had an eight-year battle with infertility—says truly got her through her ordeal. And she credits her husband with helping her to see the need for a plan.

After a year of trying to get pregnant, and then seven months on Clomid with one miscarriage under their belts, Pamela was becoming severely depressed every month when she got her period. Her husband finally picked her up and reminded her that, despite the struggle she was enduring, she still had to function. He knew her personality type needed a plan in uncertain times and encouraged her to take control by making a plan.

She did. Every month, she made a plan. And each time she failed to get pregnant, she tweaked the plan until finally, after four years, they had a son. They kept going, enduring more hope and loss, until they had a daughter, and kept going, enduring MORE hope and MORE loss, and had a second little boy. During this time, they were living in Bermuda where the cost of living was very inexpensive, and Pamela is the first to admit, they never could have afforded to keep going if they'd still lived in Canada where they were from. Pamela has emphasized how grateful she is for their financial security and recognizes not all women in her shoes are so fortunate. Along the way, they looked at adoption and donor eggs—anything that would give them the family they wanted. It just so happened, that the IVF route finally worked. And working and reworking their plan got them there.

So, how do I made a plan, you ask? One step at a time. Visualize the desired outcome. Brainstorm what needs to happen between now and that desired outcome and what you need for each step. Brainstorming may reveal people or resources you need, finances you need, knowledge you need, etc. Problem-solve. Ask one question at a time, find the answer, and execute. Wash, rinse, repeat until you have a plan or until you reach the destination. Make lists, flow-chart steps. Whatever helps YOU get organized and create some kind of a timeline to get to where you need to be. Having a plan—even the act of creating one—make me feel so much better and so much more in control of whatever is happening that I *can't* control.

So many of the people I've spoken to say that they found some bigger purpose to focus on during these hard times. Sometimes, like in Pamela's case, the challenge you're working through IS the purpose—Pamela was desperate to have children and to create a family, and so the plan she worked through was also, largely, her purpose. When my friend, Natalie's nine-and-a-half-year relationship ended, her purpose became deep self-reflection and therapy so she could understand and know herself better and truly, at a cellular level, heal from her broken relationship and her partner's infidelity and learn to trust again without the baggage of the flaws in their relationship being projected onto any new ones.

I don't think a single person I've spoken to did NOT have a mission or another purpose that helped give them something to focus on and get them through the overwhelmingly hard times. A number of the women I've spoken to started a business during their struggles. Pamela took over the infertility support group that had helped her and started helping other women.

And then there's me. When I lost my job and ten months later was still unemployed, I decided to write this book. While I was sitting in a big, fat, steaming pile of adversity, I decided to become a writer, speaker, coach—to hire my own dang self and become an entrepreneur—and teach OTHER PEOPLE how to navigate their own adversity well.

If solving your current problem IS your purpose (like for Pamela) rather than it being a survival crisis to get through, it will certainly up the stakes and raise the urgency of your plan. This can be a good thing because the motivation to get through it is "baked in." Use that motivation to your advantage and solve. the. problem.

But if that is not the case, and your adversity is more of a crisis, a threat to your survival, an uninvited guest in your life (like my unemployment situation), I can't say enough about having something else in your life—how another separate purpose will help give you a respite and a distraction and room to breathe from the overwhelm and add meaning back into your life. Seriously. When I lost my job and ten months later didn't have a new one—for the first time in my 20-year career, I felt myself sinking into the depths of worthlessness. My mission to create something or become someone who could help others saved me.

If you choose to focus on something you are passionate about, it stands to reason that it's going to bring you joy, yes? And when times are hard, what do we need more than joy? Okay, well, maybe love, but joy is high-up on the list. And this passion—this mission, it's a distraction. Distractions are great for a couple of reasons. One, obviously, it helps you to "forget" about the bad stuff for a while, and getting a break from the negative and focusing on something that brings joy is a wonderful thing. But second, have you ever tried to remember the name of something—tried and tried and tried to force it to come to you—and then, three hours later when you'd forgotten about it, it comes to you? Same concept here—sometimes part of our issue when we're facing a problem is, we are so overcome by conflicting emotions or we're overwhelmed and become paralyzed and can't make a decision or think straight—having another purpose and having that distraction sometimes comes with answers to your problem.

Caution—don't let this other, more interesting, happier, more fun purpose distract you from solving or addressing your current situation. That's called "hiding." What I am suggesting is something happy you can have to spend time on WHILE you also work your plan or your problem. So, don't fall into the avoidance trap. Do you know what sucks about avoidance? The problem remains on your plate, and you never get to move on. Life has better plans for you than that, so don't hide.

Having a purpose also gives you something to look forward to. When you are going through something terrible, I believe it's important to have things to look forward to. I have found such purpose in writing this book. And each next step in the publishing process has given me something to look forward to. Knowing I conquered the last step in the process and the anticipation of the next one has brought me so much joy. Like, wake up in the morning, excited because I get to work my dream job (that I created) today, before I think of anything else, joy. Choosing a mission and a purpose comes with the promise of joy that keeps us going, and to keep us from sinking to the lowest depths of where our minds want to sometimes take us.

When my friend Sally was diagnosed with breast cancer, they had to cancel a family vacation with her dad who lived in Trinidad (Sally and her family lived in Austin, TX), to Germany that had been planned for some time. As she went through her treatments, they talked regularly about rescheduling the trip and had it as something to look forward to. Additionally, they planned and took day trips to various places nearby when Sally's health permitted. All these things gave both Sally and her family, who was, of course, going through this adversity from their own vantage point, something to be excited about and to look forward to.

Sally passed away recently from a brain hemorrhage, and I can't help but also think that these day trips and memories she made with her family when she was able during what could have been nothing but a traumatic memory is another gift her husband and her kids were given that they can hold on to for the rest of their lives.

They don't have to be big, elaborate things, either. Sally's trips required a little more planning, but it was what they enjoyed and what THEY looked forward to. For you, maybe it's trying a new recipe, seeing a movie you've been wanting to see, or even streaming a TV show you love. Keep it simple, if simple is what's in your wheelhouse—MORE overwhelm as the result of heavy planning of elaborate things to look forward to is the opposite of what we're going for here. On the other hand, if big elaborate planning makes you happy—knock yourself out! My recommendation— find things to look forward to that make you laugh.

One other thing I'd like to say about having things to look forward to. Depending on what kind of adversity you've been through or are going through—you may not feel like putting forth the effort to plan something or to make a list of things you might like to do. Do it anyway. Do it anyway. Do it anyway. If that is how you feel, there is not much I can say to make you WANT to plan the thing. All I can say is do it anyway and keep it simple. When you do it, you'll inevitably have a good time, because you're going to choose things that, typically, you'd look forward to, right? Then, you'll keep planning and having things to look forward to and it'll get easier each time.

Another thing about overwhelm that you can't deny is a blessing in today's day and age. We are SO much more connected than we've ever been. With social media and the internet, people and information is at our fingertips. I like to tell people, Google is a fine place to start, but never diagnose a medical or psychiatric condition online.

If you think that your problem is too big or too rare and that no one is going to be able to help, you're wrong.

Information is power—be discriminating with where you find your information, consider your sources, but read, read, read. In addition to researching your issue, there is a great chance you know someone who knows someone who knows someone who can help. "Six degrees of separation" is real. Network by making a list of people you know and just ask.

I was on the advisory board of a nonprofit organization called Any Baby Can years ago. It was an organization that worked with children under the age of 12 with very rare, chronic illness and their families. There were not a lot of guardrails around the kind of support they offered—financial, resources, medical referrals, etc. They did it all.

One day, a baby named Adam was born with his bladder on the outside of his body. When his mother was told, she decided she couldn't care for him and gave him up. The hospital called the social workers at Any Baby Can who got to work looking for a foster family who could take Adam. His care was intensive—his diaper had to be changed about every 20 minutes.

One of the social workers found a family—a plumber and his wife and 16-year-old daughter—who agreed to take Adam in. Meanwhile, a surgery was identified that would correct Adam's condition. However, Medicaid deemed it cosmetic surgery and refused to pay for this life-saving surgery.

Again, the wonderful staff at Any Baby Can got involved. They petitioned a state senator's office—that senator created legislation that eventually passed, and Adam received his surgery. His foster family also fell in love with Adam and adopted him.

This situation relied on the kindness, compassion and fierce tenacity of strangers AND freaking laws to be passed in order to resolve the situation. So, again—if you think your problem is too rare or too big, you're wrong. Have hope, my friend. BIG problems get solved every day in the least likely ways.

At the end of the day, overwhelm is something that plagues us all at one time or another. Feel and process what has happened. Deal in reality. Take action. And find joy. Most of all, know this. You have done hard things before, and you can do them again. While this might be a lot, you'll get through it. Let people go through it with you. You don't have to do this alone. The sun will shine again. This, too, shall pass…

Chapter 7:
Problems We Create for Ourselves

Raise your hand if you have EVER created a problem for yourself or contributed to some kind of adversity in your life. Be honest. You can't see me right now, but I am raising my hand—high. I am the first to admit I have not always made the best choices for myself.

Remember my car accident? Okay which smart aleck just said "which one?" The one where the sweet little asshat Bambi deer ran me into a tree, and I broke all my femurs. Come on—you have to laugh sometimes, am I right?

So, around the time of that car accident, I had not been making the best nutritional choices for myself. For a while. Like, a *while*. Like so many women, after having it under control for a while, I found myself in a new season of struggle with my weight and no diet I tried was working or kept the weight off. Spoiler alert, I've since learned that is because diets don't work—you have to make nutrition a way of life, but I digress.

I was in my late thirties, and I'd convinced myself that the weight was there to stay and that this was going to be the late 30-something mom-me.

So, when this car accident happened, I ended up in a neuro-rehab hospital that had a few bells and whistles my regular doctor's office didn't have. See, as a person who can't stand, I am not able to step on a scale, and I've never found a doctor with a solution to getting my weight from me without standing. So, while I knew I was overweight, I didn't know precisely how much. Not being able to get on a scale made it soooo easy for me to lie to myself about how off-course I'd ACTUALLY gotten. What's that they say? Ignorance is bliss? Not so blissful, in my case.

Shortly after I was admitted to the neuro-rehab hospital, a super-helpful nurse wheeled a big platform into my room that I could drive my chair up onto to get my weight. Later, when I was in bed, she drove just my chair up onto it and did the math to find MY weight.

175 pounds. Stay with me, here. This chapter is IN NO WAY supposed to be a weight-shaming chapter. But here is the reality. I am five feet tall, with very little muscle tone (my point being that I couldn't even attribute any of the number to all the muscles I had from working out at the gym). I was VERY overweight and living in a body with a compromised respiratory system and atrophied muscles, so I struggled to move under good conditions. Being *this* overweight wasn't good news for my overall health and wellness.

And here's the other thing. I knew how I got there. I got there by making bad decisions. I knew what I had been eating. Turns out, I lived inside my head—no escape—and I couldn't lie to myself about how I'd gotten to be five feet tall and 175 pounds. I didn't have an underlying condition that caused me to gain weight or not to be able to lose weight. I mean, sure, I was exercise-challenged, but I could have made FAR better choices about what I had been eating and about why I was eating. I was eating to celebrate. I was eating to punish myself. I was eating because I thought I deserved it. I was eating to self-soothe. I was eating when I was sad, angry, happy, stressed, or frustrated. I was eating for Friday-night fun. Or because, Tuesday. Food had become my instant-gratification medication for whatever mood I found myself in, ever.

I don't know when I've ever been SO disappointed by something I had done to myself. I think I was in shock at first. Then, I was embarrassed. Then, I was scared. I was worried about my health. This wasn't about being cute anymore. This was real fear of what I had done to myself and how I was going to fix it.

Here is what I have learned over the years, as I've lost weight and gotten healthier. Health must be pursued. Most of us are not lucky enough, especially as we get older, to automatically have picture-perfect health. I spent a lot of time making excuses and failing to take control and take responsibility. What I'd failed to realize what that, regardless of illnesses or disabilities and physical limitations, there were things that were within my span of control. I was just making other choices. It's about acceptance and sometimes doing things you don't want to do because you believe you're worth doing the harder thing.

If you're sitting there reading these words and getting hung up on the "believe you're worth it" part, let me be the first to assure you, you are. I know that just because I say it doesn't mean you'll believe it, but again, just because you don't believe it, doesn't mean it's not true, yes? If you are a human-person, living on this earth, you have worth and are innately deserving of health and of peace of mind, and of happiness.

I've spent time in more recent years, looking for solutions to my limitations, so that I can work toward that optimal level of health for MY body. For me, even though I can't exercise, I can meditate. And I do—1-2 times a day. This is what I've found that I can do for my physical-self that keeps the toxicity of stress and anxiety under control. I CAN control what I eat—even if I don't want to. With better nutritional choices, I can improve my weight, my cholesterol, my blood sugar, my heart health, my level of hydration, my gut-heath, which improves my mood and my immune system.

I have also learned that health is a broader category than just weight that makes us a whole, healthy person—our physical health is one factor, but our mental health, our spiritual health, our relational health—these are all things I believe factor into what happens in the doctor's office, what our numbers look like and what the overall state of our health is.

This is not meant to be just a chapter on our health, though. This was ONE example. I have other examples from MY life where I made bad choices that translated into adversity for me. There are so many other ways we all do this. I also didn't work very hard in my undergraduate studies in college—I graduated, but I didn't finish with a competitive transcript or anything much to be proud of, academically, or that made me competitive from an employment perspective.

I know people who have made decisions that contributed to job loss for them. Decisions that have created excessive debt. My grandfather smoked like a chimney and that led to severe emphysema that eventually took his life. Maybe we don't participate constructively in our relationship and end up going through a divorce. So many examples.

These are all examples that are so common, and I want to reiterate, we are ALL guilty of not always making the best decisions for ourselves sometimes. The question, then, becomes, what do we do? How do we get back on track or "fix" the situation we find ourselves in?

First and foremost—Do. Not. Shame yourself. I think shame is one of the most toxic, damaging emotions you can inflict on yourself or on anyone else. I don't believe shame has any redeeming qualities. All that shame does is reinforce the suck of what you've done and perpetuate the cycle of bad behavior. Maybe because the shame leads to worthlessness and sets you on a path to more destructive behavior because you don't think you can do any better, or because you think that's the thing that will make you feel better for a minute. Shame leads to depression and anxiety. Shame leads to all kinds of bad places and not one of them that comes to mind serves any kind of constructive purpose.

In so many cases, for me, because I did something wrong, that meant I WAS wrong—wholly. THAT is what shame does to us, my friends.

I know this may be an "easier said than done" moment. Sometimes shame is something that happens whether we inflict it or not. I get it. I've been there. And of course, sometimes shame is a very natural emotion that we don't bring on intentionally. Sometimes we feel shame because *we care* that we've done something wrong, or created a problem. Let that sink in for a minute. If you *care*, that is your first sign that you are a good person with a conscience, who knows right from wrong, who wants to do better. That person doesn't deserve shame. THAT person—the one who cares enough to feel shame—deserves to be supported and empowered to make it right. That person deserves kindness and forgiveness and grace.

After you're done NOT shaming yourself, tell the truth. This can get a little tricky right here. Because sometimes when we face the truth of something we are culpable for, the tendency is to feel shame. If you do this one right, however, it can be empowering rather than shaming.

I managed teams in my corporate career for a long time. Inevitably, people on my teams did things wrong every now and then. Guess who I had on my teams? Human-people! Humans make mistakes. Some of them told the truth and owned what they did, or didn't do, that led to some kind of problem. Some didn't. I respected the hell out of the ones who owned their mistakes SO much. It's not easy to tell the truth about how you caused a problem, whether you're telling yourself or someone else. But, if you do, it can be empowering because people (and by "people," YOU inside your own mind can be one of those people) respect it. If you can give yourself respect for owning a mistake you made and making a move to correct it, that is worthy of respect…and respect leads to empowerment.

I met my best friend, Eileen, when we were working together early in my corporate life. I was still working a relatively entry-level position, trying to prove my worth and learn from people who'd been at this longer than me. Back then, I thought the worst thing that could happen was to make a mistake. And if you did, I thought the best solution was to, well, maybe not cover it up, but to try to fix it before anyone noticed.

Soon after she joined the team, I noticed something about her. She was in a much higher-level position than me. She was more educated and had been in the workforce longer than me. She was one of the smartest people I'd met who also wanted to give me the time of day. In fact, she was a natural mentor and teacher, and spent as much time as she could turning me into an analyst in our marketing division and getting me to think about what my future professional life looked like. She is the first person who got me to think seriously about going back to school for my master's degree.

But the thing I noticed was her comfort with admitting her mistakes. I sat in meetings with her and was copied on emails from her where she flatly said, "I screwed that up. My mistake. Here's the corrected info, or here is what I think we should do." Period. End of story. "I made a mistake. Here is the truth. Here is the solution." No shame. No persecution. She didn't lose her job, AND she was one of the most liked, most respected people on the team. Don't get me wrong—this was not a daily occurrence—she was very good at her job. But when she did fess-up to a mistake, it was one of the coolest moves I had seen. I respected her, and learned from her, and I followed suit, whenever I could. It became a standard to which I held myself and others on my future teams.

See, once you are sitting in the truth of what's happened (publicly OR privately) and the situation that's the current state of reality, then you can do something about it. If you never face the truth and never own a mistake, that is when you get stuck in patterns and habit loops that are bound to repeat. AND the more they repeat, the more serious the consequences may become.

But if you deal in what's real, then you can move on to first assess whether it's something that warrants correcting. Most of the time, at a minimum, I think a mistake is at least worth recognizing, learning from and not repeating. Does it mean you'll *never* repeat it…no. Is that okay? YES (okay, unless the mistake you're repeatedly making hurts someone… in those cases, I DO think a little more accountability and effort to right your wrongs is appropriate). Remember—grace, not shame, right? But awareness is the first step to maybe creating a new habit or behavior or response or pattern or learning new skills in the interest of not repeating the mistake. Again, this is where truth and honesty about what's happened and what consequences the mistake caused, is handy.

So, let's talk about that, though. Let's talk about behaviors that get us into trouble. Once you've maybe had your "come to Jesus" moment, like mine on the scale, facing a REAL number in the hospital that quantified my problem and indicated I likely had some significant health issues below the surface, I believe a constructive approach can be to get excited. Wait, what? Yup. Get excited! Change can be exciting. Change can also be hard and painful and uncomfortable and icky. BUT, if you've read *The Seven Habits of Highly Effective People,* by Stephen R. Covey, you know that one of his habits of effective people is that they begin with the end in mind. If you can see what the outcome is that you want—it can be very exciting, even if you know there is work ahead.

Think about it this way. Here we/I/you are. We've done something to contribute to some adversity in our life. You've *owned* it. You've *respected yourself* for owning it. Maybe you've even admitted your mistake(s) to others who've been impacted. (Even if your adversity isn't affecting anyone else directly, though, there are people who care about you who may be very excited to have you take them into your confidence, admit your mistake and tell them what your go-forward plan is. This little step can also create another layer of accountability for you as you do move forward to right the wrong…)

Now, you're empowered to make a change. Think about that change and what *the outcome* of that change will be. Is it a new, healthier body that you are proud of, looks great in clothes, feels energetic, yields good lab results in the doctor's office and has a healthy gut, heart, liver, will be around for years to come, etc.? Or is it a new relationship you may have yet to find, but that you know will be healthier, more authentic, more intimate one because of the changes you are prepared to make? Is it an incredible new job and career trajectory because of the work ethic you can cultivate going forward?

This is the beauty of owning our mistakes. We get to be in control again. We get to decide what the future looks like. We get to decide why that future is important to us, who we want to be in this world, what solution we want to implement and how. This is where you strike your power-pose, ladies and gentlemen.

Mistakes make us human. It's part of the experience here in this life, wearing our "Earth-suits," as my friend, Cherie, would say. We ALL make mistakes, and yes, some are on a larger scale than others. But, the bigger the mistake, the greater the opportunity for learning, AND, I believe, the bigger the opportunity to make greater and more exciting change.

Chapter 8:
Helplessness

Every. Damn. Day. Y'all.

I wake up every single day to a body that doesn't work. I can't stand. I can't walk. I can't get from the bed to my wheelchair. I can't stand in the shower. I can't get my own food out of the refrigerator. I can't pour myself a glass of water. The list of "cannots" is long, my friends. My arms can't work against gravity to reach up to fix my own hair. I can't get to the bathroom when I really, really need to, guys. I'm not trying to be gross, but I want to be very clear about just how many things I have in my life that put me at the mercy of someone else (and, frankly, the things you may do every day without considering that there are people out there who can't do those very simple, but critical things by themselves).

This is not a pity-party. This is not a play for sympathy. This is not an indictment against others who have abilities I don't have. This is merely my truth about how very helpless I am every single day of my life. When it comes to helplessness, I know what I am talking about. I rely on the Personal Care Assistants I am fortunate enough to employ, and my family to cover all my "cannots." It sucks. It's dehumanizing. It's demoralizing. It's embarrassing to have to ask your child for a glass of water—that's how helpless I sometimes am. And I hate it. That's the truth, and to say anything else would be a big, fat lie. I also accept that these are my circumstances. I'll come back to that in a minute…Because, to further illustrate my breadth and depth of experience in this area, I want to tell you about a different kind of helplessness I experienced this past year. It's one thing to be helpless in your own circumstances, but it's quite a different experience to be helpless as an onlooker to someone you love's circumstances, and I (like, I'm sure, so many of you) have seen it from both sides.

In 2020, my dad lost his leg and hip after something like 15 years of progressively worsening health from a faulty hip replacement. Last year, he spent more time in the hospital than not. During the outbreak of COVID, no less. I couldn't see him or be there to hold his hand as he became disabled and wheelchair-bound.

There is so much trauma weaved into this 15-year story for both of my parents, but out of respect for them and their privacy, I will leave it at this. It is really not my story to tell, but my point in bringing it up is that I also know the feeling of not being able to fix something or make something better when someone you love is suffering.

I don't know if there have been words invented to describe how helpless I felt (and still sometimes feel now as they try to find their new normal) when I spoke to either of my parents on the phone last year. It is ironic that, he is one half of the team that raised me. He and my mom, together, raised me to be strong and to find humor, to count my blessings and to make the best of a crappy situation. He helped me believe I was amazing, even if I had to "do me" from a wheelchair. I wanted and want so badly to be able to help him see the same thing about himself, and I see now what a difficult job that was for my parents. It is so hard to know what to say to ease the burden, to take the pain and sorrow away, to give hope back. It is so hard to know what to do. Especially in a crazy time when you can't even be in someone's presence or even bring them groceries because #pandemic. Even the box of popsicles I thought would be a treat for him weren't allowed. One day, I took them to the rehab hospital he was in for a while after the amputation to just drop them off, knowing I wouldn't be allowed in. I AND the contraband were turned away. (I am shaking my metaphorical fist at YOU, Coronavirus!).

Though I know they would say this isn't true, a phone call or email or eCard felt insignificant and almost futile in the face of the massiveness of the traumatic experience he and my mom have gone through.

I would imagine many of you know what I am talking about. 2020 gave thousands, if not millions, of us reasons to feel helpless. As a person who probably would have ended up on a ventilator and may never have ever come off of it, just the threat of COVID made me feel like a sitting duck every single day. I had nightmares about not being able to breathe. You can make your bubble as tight as you are able, but things and people (in my case, my PCAs) still had to come in and out and I knew I was not 100% protected. It was out of my control.

Besides that, people lost jobs. Lost their lives. Sickness. Financial stress. And beyond the year of COVID, there are natural disasters that have devastated entire cities and beyond. Business decisions that are out of your hands but will have direct impacts on you and your families. Having a sick child. Have I hit on your circumstance yet? I know this is a very small list of potential situations and you may be facing something else that makes you feel equally helpless.

Here is what I know about MY circumstances. Let's talk about the one that put me in a wheelchair and has taken SO much control away from me in my own physical body.

I can't change it.

Knowing this is the key to getting my control back. I'm not saying that in terms of getting my *abilities* back, but I can take the *control* back.

I can fight and flail and cry and be angry and play the "what if" game in my head. I can be miserable, and I can focus on the humiliation of needing another person to do things for me that should be our God-given right to do for ourselves, as *humans*.

I can be a victim. I can make everyone around me unhappy. I can complain incessantly. I can remind everyone I know on a daily basis how hard my life is and how it sucks to be me. I can become a horrible human being who feels so sorry for myself all the time that I drive everyone away. I can do that. It's a choice. It's one way to go.

What a miserable existence that would be. Granted, the picture I painted is extreme, but I have known a person or two in my time who chose this excessive victimization over happiness and acceptance. I've also known people who have chosen varying degrees of this victimization.

That's the thing though. There was *one* event in my life that is at the root of ALL of this—my diagnosis of the illness that puts me in a wheelchair. That day, I was a victim of that diagnosis and of what it meant. It was out of my control, and I was helpless to it. But I have a whole life beyond that day and that event that caused my circumstances. The rest of the days, I simply live with the circumstances and the by-products that diagnosis created.

To live out the sorrow and the misery and the suffering day in and day out, THAT would be a choice I make, and that choice would continue to make me a victim OF MY OWN DOING. If that were how I lived my life—in misery—and someone came to me one day and said, "wow, you seem so unhappy. How did this happen?" And I said, "well, see, 46 years ago I was diagnosed with a condition that put me in a wheelchair…" Bullshit! That's not what was making me miserable. I would be what was making me miserable. Every day for the past 46 years, waking up and choosing to victimize myself again and again for something that happened 46 YEARS AGO! Something that can't be changed. Something that sucks, but that I do have a choice around how to feel about it and how to live with it. And that, I might add, I've done pretty well.

I'm getting a little riled up, here, but I have some very, very strong feelings about how we victimize ourselves in times when we feel wronged, when something has gone wrong and when we feel helpless. It's a trigger, for sure, and like I've said before, ride that wave of emotion. And then, let it go. *Accept* that this is where you are and that maybe you can't change it. But, dangit, we CAN control how we respond.

Who do you want to show up as in this life? I know who I want to show up as—I want to be courageous, kind, able to find humor. I want to show up as someone who is grateful, someone who focuses on solutions rather than problems. I want to be someone other people want to be around. I want to be someone people respect. I want to be someone people said was brave and good-natured and positive. I want to be someone I can look in the mirror and be proud of who I showed up as that day. I'm sure I am making this all sound very easy, but this is a lifetime of learning and of being a person who has had a TON of opportunity to reflect on and evolve in how I navigate a crap-ton of challenges. I am the first to say, I haven't always shown up well, but I've worked hard to be intentional and to find the good and live my challenges out in a way that gives even more meaning to my life.

It's times like these when things go wrong and when we are made to feel helpless that hand us our humanity, challenge our resolve and test us. I haven't always passed these tests, but I am failing less and less as time goes by and I can practice these skills and be mindful about who I am in these moments.

So yes, all this to say that *acceptance* is critical. It won't change your circumstances, but it can sure make them more livable.

The other things that have helped me in my daily struggles with help-lessness are closely tied to who I want to show up as in the world. All those things I mentioned are what gets me through it. I am so *grateful* for my family and for the Personal Care Assistants I have who show up daily and enable me to live my life. Many of them have become dear friends who I still call on long after their employment with me ends to cover a shift here and there when someone is sick or on vacation. I *laugh* daily at the ridiculousness of the situations we find ourselves in.

True story—I had just hired a brand-new care assistant and she was with me for one of her first shifts. I have this thing called a patient lift (or a Hoyer lift) to get me from, say, my wheelchair to the bed. The bedroom had fairly thick carpet and steering the lift across the room was proving to be a bit of a challenge for her. As she "heave-hoe'd," she sort of grunted, "bitch shit!"

I looked at her, raised my eyebrows and said quietly, "did you just say 'bitch-shit?" She looked at me sheepishly and we both broke into hysterics. Would it be easier to have legs that carried me from a chair to the bed? Heck-yes! Would I prefer that? Definitely. Would I prefer not to have to hire and fire and manage care assistants and pay their salary out of my own pocket? You betcha! But the reality was, I was dependent on her and dependent on this lift. I could have been angry and annoyed by the cumbersome process and by the struggle. But that is not who I want to show up as in this world. Instead, I couldn't help but realize when I heard the ridiculous phraseology that erupted from underneath her physical strain, that we were probably about to be best friends—and it was one of the funniest moments ever.

I get up every single day and I strive to do it better and better. When something goes wrong, I am quick to jump to *solutions* rather than dwelling on the *problem*. That mindset is what gets me through each and every day as a happy person I am proud to be. All of it is what makes me feel more in control when my circumstances deem me helpless.

So now I feel like I want to move on to try to help us all make sense of those moments when we feel helpless to help someone we love. I feel like there is an additional layer of complexity to this one. Honestly, I can take control and make sense out of my own situation all day long. But when it's someone I love? Harder.

I spoke to a lot of people leading up to writing this book and it felt like something that universally challenges people. Everyone generally agreed that it's easier to make sense of and respond to their own challenging circumstances. The "fixer" in us all struggle with not being able to take the pain away for someone close to us.

So, let's focus on some tactics. There are a lot of insights I got from people who were onlookers of someone else's hardship, OR in asking them in their own times of adversity, what they wish someone would have done for them.

Honestly, the first one is just to be present. I have not always done a good job of this myself, because, if I am being honest, I think I under-valued the power of just being with someone, letting them know I was thinking of them and that I cared. As a "fixer," anything that didn't fix the problem at hand felt useless. It's not. Where I went wrong is that I was thinking about it from a standpoint of what it gave ME rather than THEM. Let *that* sink in for a second…I wanted to fix the problem and if I couldn't, nothing else was good enough. But it shouldn't have been about what I wanted. The other person, of course, knows you can't fix their problem. I couldn't save my dad's leg and hip, and he knew that. But knowing you matter—that your suffering matters—to someone, I think that's probably worth a lot more than I gave it credit for. The emails or the phone calls I mentioned earlier may have felt insignificant to *me*… but it wasn't about me. The other person wants to know that they are worth people praying for and spending 20 minutes on the phone with, listening. I wish I had done more of it for my dad AND for my mom.

No one wants to feel like a burden. This is another theme that came up again and again and again. Several people told me that it was hard for them to accept help, and so they were a strong proponent of just doing what you were going to do for someone without asking for permission. In fact, some said that when they were in the thick of their problem, they couldn't have answered a question like "what can I do?" If you are going to make them dinner—just make dinner and drop it off. If you are going to mow their lawn, show up on Saturday with your mower and go at it. If you're going to make them a care package, throw it all in a cute basket and drop it off.

Sure, there are other things people might need where you do need permission or to coordinate—taking them to a doctor's appointment, going grocery shopping for them, picking their kids up from school. Figure out how to make the collaboration as easy as possible for them, and then follow through.

As hard as this nut is to crack, the net of what I've learned in life and in talking to others about how to help someone else takes me back to Maslow's hierarchy of needs, which I know I've mentioned in other chapters, but if we are talking about overcoming challenges in life, I feel like this theory is a good one to help us problem-solve. And, if we look at the layers of Maslow's hierarchy, physiological needs (food, water, clothes, shelter, air), love and human connection, esteem (which includes attention and self-esteem) and security are all very significant human needs.

When you are going through a really difficult time, I personally believe that short of being able to solve a person's problem (and if you can, or if you have a resource available to you that can be useful, obviously, you step up) if we keep these basic human needs in mind and look for ways to help that reinforce those very basic needs, that might be the key.

Think about what you can do for them to help them ensure that they are fed, clothed, and have a roof over their head, that they feel safe, secure, loved, needed, wanted, valued and worthy of your time.

The truth is, we are all human and we all have times where we are taken out of our element and our ability to help ourselves is compromised. All of us. At one time or another—maybe when you're 1, maybe when you're 81, but I think a time will come for all of us when we face this first-hand, and probably many more times where you experience it second-hand.

Don't be a victim. It's bad enough when our control is taken away and we face a challenge we didn't cause or expect. Don't further victimize yourself by staying stuck in a mindset of helplessness. Your body might be—but your mind isn't. And that is the more critical piece. We get to decide how we show up and who we are even under the most difficult of circumstances. That is what makes or breaks a life experience.

Mindset is also key when it is someone you love who has a problem you can't solve.

Know your limitations. As much as you might want to fix their problem, you may not be able to.

So, remember; it's not about you. Don't make it about you and what makes you feel better. If you want to help, think about *their* needs and how you can help fill those needs. That is all anyone can ask of us—it's all you can ask of yourself.

Chapter 9:
Job Loss

I hate to keep referencing COVID, but it was such an event in our world for the past year with such massive consequences, and still is not completely behind us. One of the BIGGEST bits of fallout from the pandemic was job loss. SO MANY lost their jobs. And we all know that with job loss comes the suckiness of financial stress and insecurity, which comes with all kinds of secondary consequences to us and to our families and our ability to take care of them. It comes with insecurity, and fear. It can cause us to doubt our ability, our LIKEABILY, our skills—it can really do a number on our self-worth and confidence. I am a solid member of this club—I've earned my badges.

When I lost my job three years ago, it was pre-COVID. I was laid off from my previous company of six and a half years when that company was acquired. The decision was made to open a new office in Lithuania to reduce cost of doing business, and the company re-hired for a number of our operations over there. Though I hear Vilnius, Lithuania is beautiful, this is more of a move than I or my family wanted. Because the company was in full-on cost-cutting mode, there was not a lot of alternate hiring going on in my immediate location and so I took the severance package they offered me, believing I was highly employable and fearing NOT that I would have any trouble finding a job.

Confession. I was actually even a little bit excited. Instead of feeling angry or sad about it at the time, I felt recharged by possibility and of what was to come, where I would end up and what I'd be doing. The worst part was having to lay off my team. I wasn't worried about myself, but the impact to them and to their families weighed on me.

Once the severance was complete, ten months went by. This is the truth. I'd been a department manager. I was making a six-figure salary. I had over 15 years of software experience, and a consistent record of advancement at every company where I'd ever worked. I'd always received strong performance reviews. I was connected and knew people at every software company in Austin, Texas that you could possibly want to work for. I have a master's degree. That all added up to great confidence that I would land an even better job than I was leaving.

In those ten months, I applied for 341 jobs. I interviewed for 53 unique jobs. Those are not typos. I worked my butt off to try to get a job. If we break down the math across the timeline, that looks like 34 jobs applied for per month, or a little over one a day, including weekends. AND, more than five unique jobs interviewed for per month—or one and a quarter *new* job interviews a week. A few of those jobs didn't go further than the first call with the recruiter (I can remember three off the top of my head). But the vast, VAST majority of them consisted of between two and five interview rounds before it was all said and done. If you multiply those 50 jobs by a minimum of two, that's 100 interviews in ten months—now, multiply by sometimes three, four or five???

That's a crap-ton of interviewing (yes, "crap-ton" is a valid metric). So much, I had to sit with it for a second when I broke it all down.

NOW if you consider that I received 53 either hard rejections, or notifications that the position had gone to an internal hire, or that the position had been frozen at the 13th hour, or that I'd been "ghosted," conservatively, once a week, FOR TEN MONTHS, it begins to make sense that I *did finally* begin to feel a little sorry for myself and the fear started creeping in. After all, for every single one of those 53 jobs, if you consider all the time, energy, work and *hope* one puts into every single one, it's no wonder I finally hit a wall and my usually pretty positive thoughts got a little darker.

I had my "bathroom floor" moment (Metaphorically. My inability to stand prevents me from getting out of my chair and sinking oh-so-dramatically to the floor, and my thoughts weren't dark enough yet to have me fling myself to the floor—that tile is HARD!!). But suffice it to say, I was in the bathroom—I'd just washed my hair and was staring at myself in the mirror, trying to make sense of *any* of it.

After a third interview with a company I believed wanted me more than any other I had spoken to, I received an email from the recruiter letting me know that the position was being temporarily put on hold, pending budget timelines. She also said that the VP I'd spoken to had requested more resumes once the position DID open back up. Therefore, reading between the lines, I was NOT the slam-dunk I thought I was. Dangit. Sonofa…

The practical, responsible side of me began to panic. We'd been fortunate so far—I don't know a lot of people who could afford to be out of work for more than ten months and have enough cash reserves to stay afloat. AND, by my calculations, we'd still be okay for another 5-6 months, if we were careful. But my severance and our savings WOULD NOT last forever. Would we need to sell our house? What about my daughter's tuition? She was scheduled to start college in nine days (yes, NINE days)! When your security is threatened, your mind has the capacity to go to very dark places.

I spent much of that afternoon and evening feeling nauseous. Wondering what I was doing wrong. Feeling inadequate. Second-guessing my intelligence, my communication style, my abilities, my personality. I was feeling hopeless.

Hopeless. There it is. It's the f-bomb of adversity. It is a word I've stricken from my own personal vocabulary in my life. I have used it in the past, and it makes me cringe. It's a word I don't believe has any place in any of our mouths. So that night, when my brain started to go to very dark places, and I could no longer see a future of prosperity and paid bills, when my mind threatened to give up, to reject the practice of showering and I wanted to just sleep for the next month, it scared me.

That was THE moment. I heard the thoughts in my head, and they sickened me. I realized that right there, in that moment, I had a decision to make. I could either become the worst version of myself and become this angry, frustrated, jaded person, OR, I could write a book. THIS book. A book about overcoming adversity while I sat in a very large pile of it myself.

I didn't stop looking for work right away, but I suddenly had a new mission. I had an *additional* mission—and that new mission saved my bacon. It gave me a place to pour out everything I knew I was, every other piece of adversity I've ever experienced and ALL I've learned from it, and it could be like therapy. As I've written, it has solidified my values, my belief of who I am and of what I am capable of. It gave me purpose. It gave me something that would, ironically, also take the spotlight off myself and my own problems—even though they were the subjects of this book—and allowed me to create something for YOU. Something that would help you and, I hope, allow you to move on from or move through whatever YOU may be going through. Something that would help you find yourself, define your own values and that would help you show up in your life as the person you also *know* that you are. Something that maybe even would help you help someone you love who is struggling.

Job loss. It sucks. It takes so much control away from us. But what I've learned with ALL certainty, is that no matter what, we are still in control, we can learn from it and we can master our mindset as we go through it. More on this in a minute, but first, I have another story to share…

I *wish* I could say the story I just told was my only experience I've had with unemployment, but I can't. When I was 28, I lost my job. I'd been with my company for seven years and was working as an analyst in the marketing department. I had absolutely no formal training as an analyst, but when the department reorganized, they assigned me to this role with a sr. analyst who'd been assigned to mentor and train me. It was amazing. Remember my best friend, Eileen? She was the best teacher I'd ever had, and I loved going to work and learning from her. Then, one day, she transferred to another department. I was devastated—what would I do?

I didn't know how to be an analyst without her yet. I'd learned so much from her, but was nowhere near self-sufficient. Her replacement was very nice and a talented analyst, but didn't seem as though she had been tasked with being a mentor to me or continuing my training.

Over time, I did very, very basic work that was assigned to me, but my deliverables and reports were nothing spectacular. I didn't find any exciting trends, or mine any data or report any miraculous outcomes of anything. I didn't build fancy models or offer insights or even any interesting information. I was feeling insecure and I'd checked out.

Let's be real. I *could have* asked for help. I *could have* done research. I *could have* studied on my own. But I didn't. I gave up. I coasted, and I did *nothing* to help myself.

Then, one day I went into work, and the rumors were flying. People were being laid off. The mood in the building was somber. And then, my phone rang. My boss needed to see me in the conference room. I knew immediately. And, sure enough, my position had been cut and it was to be my last day. I can still see the faces of the people—my coworkers, my friends, peering over the top of their cubicles, watching my boss escort me from the conference room to my desk to pack up my things. It was humiliating.

What was worse, I was largely responsible. Though my boss said it wasn't—she said they had to cut the analyst function by 50%. There were two of us, and I was the more junior one. Deep down, though, I knew there were things I should have done differently. I felt like such a failure. I didn't admit it then, but looking back, it was my fault. Gag. I *hate* saying this. I've never admitted this to anyone and it's painful to admit, but it's the truth. I am admitting it now, for you. For the sake of all of our learning. Double-gag. Back then, I was young. It was the first company I'd ever worked for. I didn't have the world experience I have now to give me the ability to own what I should have owned.

Here's what I *did* do. I kept my secret (that it was my fault), but I learned. I was accountable—even if just to myself. I vowed to myself to never put myself in this position again. When I got my next job, my work ethic was solid. I took it seriously, and I worked hard.

It was a pivotal time in my life, and I learned a very important lesson. I learned to take responsibility. Even if I didn't declare my failure or my culpability publicly, I learned to look at my shortcomings and was the best employee that next company could have asked for. And because of that, my career took off. I was promoted three times in eight years. I got my first job as a manager. All this because I went through this hard time—that I caused—but I was accountable to myself.

There it is. Two job losses, two completely different scenarios—one I believe I caused, one I know I didn't. Learnings galore!

One thing I'd like to call out here—taking responsibility does not require us to heap shame upon ourselves. Knowing I'd contributed to my job loss the first time around—of course, I beat myself up a little. I'm human. But what was more noteworthy here was that, I *cared*. The regret and the shame we sometimes feel over things we've done wrong are indicators that we are actually good people. If we didn't care or feel any shame and moved on without any reflection whatsoever, we might be sociopaths. Or psychopaths. I don't know…some kind of "path." You see where I am going. Caring and wishing we'd done better is a *good* trait to have.

But don't allow it to be paralyzing. If used properly, it can become the tool it was for me to move forward and to do better the next time. And I did. I knew my performance wasn't going to impress anyone else and I wanted a successful career I could be proud of. From this experience I learned that I needed to work harder, to be more accountable for my own success. I was still single at the time, but I knew that maybe next time, if I didn't get it together and do better, maybe I'd have a spouse or a family I'd also be disappointing. I knew I needed to commit to not just my success, but the success of the next company I worked for. It absolutely served as the motivation I needed to improve myself and to transform who I showed up as professionally before the stakes got even higher. I didn't want this to be a pattern I repeated or a theme in my life.

By this time, I'd given up music and gone back to grad school because I knew I had to set myself up for success to have the life and the security I wanted. I was walking the walk by trying to improve my general education and to position myself for advancement, but I also needed to put my work ethic where my mouth was in my daily job.

So, like I said. Care, yes. Desire to do better, yes. Learn, yes. *Actually* do better, yes. Don't wallow to the point of paralysis. Take action—this is where we get our control back and we, once again, become the architects of our own lives.

That was the common denominator between the two times I've lost my job. I took control—of my response, of my thoughts, of my mindset, and of my actions. I think that with something like losing your job, where the aftershocks can be SO huge, not only to our security, but to our identity and our self-confidence, there is too much at stake to not be methodical.

Step 1—I 100% say, evaluate reality. Look objectively at how you got here. What feedback did your employer give you? Do you own some of the responsibility? If you do, take that feedback or that information as a gift! Use it and improve! Sure, there is some sting that comes along with that; I've been there, and it sucks. But, if you can own *how* you may have contributed to your circumstances, you will respect yourself. There is definitely something freeing in knowing where you didn't shine. Especially if you use that knowledge as motivation to do better, and you commit to doing better. If there is a skill or a competency you are lacking, there is no blame in that. There is a little bit if you know it and you don't do anything about it. So, learn. Improve. Impress yourself and you will impress others.

If you didn't create or contribute to your circumstances, *know* that. It will maybe help take some of the emotion out of it if, truly, all it was was a business decision. You can still learn and improve—take inventory of your skills and competencies anyway. We can all ALWAYS improve. Look for areas where you can do and be better and where you can up your game. But also, take inventory of where you kick butt, and know you will keep doing it. Reinforce that knowledge by asking for recommendations on LinkedIn. Try not to depend on the external validation, but go ahead and take some comfort in the fact that you can get it, if you do.

Regardless of which of these scenarios are yours, there is emotion and baggage that comes along with being told one day that you are no longer required. It hurts—let yourself sit with those feelings of loss and hurt. It's okay not to be okay for a minute. You will know when you've spent enough time grieving and are ready to move on. AND, you will know if you are wallowing and becoming depressed. That is the time when maybe you begin to push yourself a little to decide who you want to be and start showing up that way, and/or get some help. Talking to someone while going through this is NEVER wrong.

Step 2—Take action.

Tactically AND with respect to your mindset. Like I said in step 1— figure out who you already are, decide who you want to be (PS—it may be the exact person you already are) and BE that person. Show up every day with that intentionality and fight for what you want. Make decisions and interact with people in a way you'll feel good about when your head hits the pillow at night.

Gratitude is HUGE! Make sure you are recognizing the things in your life you have to be grateful for every single day. I've had a practice of writing down a few things I am grateful for every day for a few years. Reminder—if you know you're going to ask yourself every day what you are grateful for, you will go through your life looking for things to be grateful for. And, when you look for things to be grateful for, you find them. Remember, you can have things in your life that suck, and at the same time, there are ALWAYS things that are wonderful—and true.

Let yourself get excited about what lies ahead. Is it a shiny new career that is bigger and better than what you had? (PPS—it very well might be!) Do you want to take the opportunity to pivot and try going in a slightly (or hugely) different direction? If you do, figure out what needs to happen to make that possible. For me, my *second* and most recent unemployment led to entrepreneurship and a passion career that I am grateful to wake up to every day. It's been hard work, but I have never been happier. I've become a motivational speaker, a writer, a coach, a podcast host, and an advocate for disability awareness. So, get excited, and get to work. Cast a wide net and see what happens. BE OPEN. Opportunities come to us when we have an open heart and an open mind. Something may come along that it didn't even occur to you to hope for.

Reflect. Mourn. Find gratitude. KNOW who you are and who you want to be. Get excited. Take action. Be open. Ask for what you want—even if you think it's crazy and is totally out of the question, you might get it. Have hope. This could be the beginning of the best chapter of your life, yet.

Chapter 10:
Shame

How much time do we have? This is a big subject. I feel like I should go fuel up on a bowl of Wheaties…nope, too late, my writing fingers are twitching (also, there's not a Wheatie in the house!). Let's do this!

College. Oy. How many things do we get wrong when we're 18-22 years old? This is not a rhetorical question. I got plenty of things wrong when I was in college. It's funny—you think you know it all back then, but you soooooooo don't.

I was in a sorority in college. I was a Delta Zeta (DZ), and I loved it. But I want to share one, short little five-minute experience with you from this time that I have *never* stopped feeling badly about. It was my senior year of college, and one of the traditions at the end of every DZ's last year was to address the chapter at a gathering at the house and tell them what you were going on to do once you graduated and to give some advice or say something inspiring. Yeaaaahhhh. I was one of the last to go because I'd been on the phone during most of it in the other room handling a crisis over the salary I'd be making at the job I'd accepted. I am sorry to say, my swansong from DZ—the last time I saw SO many of these women—went something like this…

"I'm sorry I've been out of the room for most of this—you can probably tell from my teary face that I've been on a phone call that was upsetting. Turns out, the job I accepted and will be starting in the next few weeks is going to pay $7 an hour (this was 1995, by the way). Not sure how I'll pay for rent or anything else, but that's how the cookie crumbles. So, hey, in case any of you were wondering what you'll be worth at the end of all your school, that's about it. Thanks for the fun, the friendship, and the memories."

Oh. My. Dear. Lord. I almost couldn't make myself finish typing that. I'm so embarrassed. Be honest. You're thinking about that thing you've been feeling shame over and feeling really, really good about yourself right now, aren't you? Honestly, I don't know how I managed to get those words out of my mouth, they were so ugly and demoralizing to everyone in the room. In that moment, I think I would have easily been voted "*Least* Likely to Become a Motivational Speaker or Writer of Personal Development." If anyone is reading this who was in that room on that day and remembers this horror—please accept my apology.

The only thing that has given me even the tiniest little bit of respite from the shame is knowing how young I was, how dramatic we could be at that age, and how shocked I was by what I'd just learned on the phone call I had right before I had to speak. Honestly, I was freaking out. I felt disappointed and a little trapped. I didn't realize I had options. I didn't realize that budgeting was real and that as a single person, I was going to be okay and would make it work.

My parents had helped me get the job through someone they knew at the company, and I didn't want to disappoint them. Even so, I have NEVER stopped feeling ashamed of what I said to those girls that day. Honestly, it made me sick *even* when I said it, in the moment, but I said it anyway.

Another time, when my daughter was about six, we were hanging out. Something fell on the floor, and as she bent down to pick it up, she sighed, rolled her eyes and exclaimed, "Dangit!" I looked at her, partially amused and partially unamused, and asked her where she had heard that word. I mean, it wasn't an f-bomb, but it isn't a cute word coming out of a six-year-old's mouth, either. She started to cry. I told her right away, that it was okay, but I wanted to know where she'd heard it. After I got her to stop crying, she said, "You." Ouch. Shame-punch in the face. Newsflash.

This wasn't the last time I was less than proud of my parenting example or performance. I mean, I think I've been a pretty good parent, but I've had more than the one moment that was, well, cringey. Shame, shame, shame, shame, shame...

Then, there are bigger, deeper examples from my life where I'd have to bring in a therapist to help us truly and sufficiently deconstruct the shame—being unable to control my weight and my eating and feeling too ashamed of how I looked to want to be in photos—"hi, shame." Things I've done or said in friendships that have caused us to drift apart—shame. Not paying my parents or other family enough attention—double-shame. Not spending NEARLY enough time with my grandmother before she passed away. So. Much. Shame. Losing jobs, whether my fault or not. SHAME! Poor grades in undergrad studies. More shame.

I've felt shame over my disability. About being different than other people. I have felt shame for inconveniencing people or for being a burden (my word, not theirs!) when I've needed help. I've felt shame when joining a group of people for a social outing and the logistics or destination need to be modified to meet *my* needs. When—at the company I worked at for seven years where I was the only person with physical limitations, when they wanted to have a corporate outing and needed to choose an activity with no physical requirements because of me, one single person out of 700. I felt shame for commandeering the event and believing they'd all rather be axe-throwing or golfing.

When I was a department manager for that very company, once a quarter (if all went well), I was given budget to take my team out for a fun outing. I saw other managers taking their teams rock-wall climbing, or to do other, quite physical things. I'd always ask my team what they wanted to do, and I cringed as I saw their wheels turning and knew they were having conversations about what would be accessible for me. What should have been a reward *for them, and only them,* turned into a debate about what would accommodate *me.* We always ended up going to a movie and, if I had enough budget leftover, to lunch or dinner. I felt bad. I mean, I *know* leaving work for the day and going to a movie isn't a hardship, but I knew it wasn't interesting or original, or anything they couldn't do on their own time, either. They always had fun with each other and thanked me for the outing, but sometimes, I wondered if they wished they had a different manager who could take them to do something—*anything* else on those days. Not because of anything they said or did, but because, well, shame.

Just last night, I had a sleepless night because I was horribly uncomfortable and having some pain. I can't turn over, or reposition myself in bed, and had to wake my husband up four or five times for help. Every single time, I laid there, *each time*, for an extra 15-60 minutes before waking him up because I just felt so bad.

Here's the deal. Shame is something that I think affects us all, if we have a conscience, at one time or another in life. Why? Because nobody's perfect. We all have problems. We all make mistakes, and like I've said before, if we care about ourselves, our reputation or about other people, shame is a natural emotion to feel. Also, though, shame is ugly. It's often misplaced or over-exaggerated. And it's so mean—the things we say to ourselves during these shame spirals. Yuck. Clearly, I do it—even though I know how flawed and icky this thing is that I'm telling myself. Sometimes, yes, I deserve to have some remorse, like that god-awful departing speech I left my sorority with. But not always. Sometimes, I deserve a hug for the pain I am in that is being replaced with this misguided shame.

Let's take a minute and look at the actual definition of shame. It's such a big, prevalent monster, I think it'll be helpful.

My old friend, Merriam-Webster, first served-up this definition: a painful emotion caused by consciousness of guilt, shortcoming, or impropriety.

That almost explains or defines what I've talked about to this point, but it leaves out the misplaced shame we sometimes feel for things that are out of our control. So, I kept looking, and found this definition from Wikipedia, of all places. But the distinction is that the word is defined in the context of "shame in psychology." It says, "**Shame** is an unpleasant self-conscious emotion typically associated with a negative evaluation of the self; withdrawal motivations; and feelings of distress, exposure, mistrust, powerlessness, and worthlessness."

There we go—"negative evaluation of the self." That is exactly it. In these situations, we are evaluating ourselves and the judgement we are making is that we are *wrong* somehow. Not just a thing we've done, but what or who we are, or what that thing we did *means we are*. We are judging it to be wrong or negative and then feeling bad about it. Whether right or wrong.

Literally, the thought that came to mind after I wrote that last sentence was, "Jeez. There is so much to feel bad about in this life and in the world. Why would we *go looking for* more things to feel bad about? Things that are out of our control anyway?"

Where is Brene Brown when you need her? Seriously—if I heard ANYONE else say they laid in bed in pain for an hour because they felt shame over not being able to move their leg and needed to wake their husband up to help, I would tell them in earnest how inappropriately that shame was being placed. You can't help needing that person in that moment, and if they are there, and if they love you, and if they are willing to help, why shouldn't you just let them and feel grateful to have them? That is what I'd say to the other person, so why are the rules different for me? Because shame is a natural human inclination. Shame happens to us all. And shame sucks.

Mally Roncal of Mally Beauty attended a mastermind group of women I am helping to lead this quarter and she came to speak about Imposter Syndrome, which falls squarely in the shame category. I loved how she talked about it. At one point, she said, "It's a sneaky little bastard that likes to show up at the most inopportune times." It's true! Shame shows up when it's not invited, not warranted, and serves no purpose. Sometimes, it sneaks in the back door and we don't see it coming until we're swimming in it.

There is, however, another word that's coming to mind. Remorse. Remorse feels like a more constructive verb. Let's check out the difference between shame and remorse by comparing the definitions. Here is how Merriam-Webster defines remorse—"a feeling of being sorry for doing something bad or wrong in the past : a feeling of guilt." See, remorse feels healthy to me. It's about feeling badly about something you maybe should feel bad for, not about evaluating and judging who and what we *are*. Shame is more toxic. Don't get me wrong, I think remorse, can be taken too far, but if someone feels remorse for something they did or said that *was* wrong, that's appropriate (no one wants to be a narcissist who never makes a mistake and never feels bad about anything).

I mentioned Brene Brown earlier, who is one of the foremost experts on shame (and vulnerability). I came across a definition she uses for shame—**shame** is an "intensely painful feeling or experience of believing that we are flawed and therefore unworthy of love and belonging." Oh, Brene. You totally get me!

Brene's definition is in alignment with what I've been saying about judgement or belief that we ARE flawed, not that we did something flawed and need to apologize. If we do something wrong, it doesn't mean we ARE wrong. It was the thing we did or said. That doesn't mean we're not good people. It doesn't mean we are not worthy of love. It doesn't mean we need to be condemned to a life of shame and feeling bad about what we did and who we are as humans.

In her book *Daring Greatly,* Brene also says, "shame derives its power from being unspeakable…if we cultivate enough awareness about shame, to name it and to speak it, we've basically cut it off at the knees."

So, there is a remedy for shame. Eh, Brene? Shame, to me, and kind of like Mally said, is a subversive little creature. I have a vision coming to mind of a little cartoon monster that is sketched messily in charcoal. No color, because it lurks and blends with the shadows. It creeps around and pokes at you like a coward, demanding that you disapprove of yourself and then hides in the shadows while you secretly blame and shame yourself in your mind, relentlessly, about this thing you did and how that makes you unworthy of taking up space.

But, in my mind, when we name this little creature (I'm going to call mine Bob) I'm seeing a light switch turn on in the cartoon and suddenly, Bob is not black and white and grey. He's blue and dark green and a little yellow. He's a character that is more than the badness I feel for what I did. Bob becomes a complicated ball of more cuddly emotions worthy of nurturing and forgiving.

It's interesting—I am clearly not cured of shame. I experienced it as recently as last night. BUT. I think that what Brene says about talking about shame, calling it out and naming it, is spot-on (I know that my approval of her 20 years of research is exactly what she's been waiting for). Writing this chapter has almost been a bit of an experiment of her diagnosis of shame. As I've written about the things I feel or have felt shame over, I've felt a weight lift. I have been able to rationalize some things I've been looking at purely out of charged emotion. I don't feel shame now for any of the scenarios I've shared with you. I feel regret, and I feel sorry, and I wish I hadn't done them. But I don't think I am unworthy of being.

I know I am a good person and that the good things I do and have done FAR outweigh the bad. I've made mistakes, yes. I've hurt people, yes. But I know that doesn't make me bad. It makes me human. I challenge anyone to get through life without hurting someone or making a mistake. It's impossible. But, when we do those things, it doesn't automatically erase our "good."

So, I encourage you also, to turn the light on your "Bob." Say his name and share with a trusted friend what you are feeling badly about. They will help you see that #1, we can never undo what we've done, so in the interest of our mental (and physical) health, you have to find a way to feel better about it—to let it go. And that #2, what you did or said doesn't make you a bad person—you had a bad moment that could have been influenced or informed by 100 different things and you made a bad choice.

Make amends. Apologize if you can. Maybe too much time has passed—maybe time is not a factor. Maybe the person isn't around to apologize to, like my grandmother. In that case, it's up to you to forgive yourself. I love a definition of forgiveness I heard Oprah say once, "Forgiveness is letting go of the wish that what happened was different than what it was." Let it go and do better.

I'm going to stick with Brene here—she is SO wise, and also says, "Grace means that all of your mistakes now serve a purpose instead of serving shame." You know me—I am all about finding purpose in a situation! In the case of shame and things we are holding on to that we feel excessively bad about and that cause us to question our worthiness, I think that every single time, it can serve to help us do better. We can learn from our mistakes—I don't like feeling the way I do when I do or say something wrong. That alone—the not wanting to feel that way—can be a deterrent. It can help us behave better in the future.

Hurting someone can serve a purpose, if we learn from it (I'm not saying to go out and look for ways to hurt people so you can learn a lesson, but if you DO hurt someone on life's journey, please learn from it). It can teach us empathy. It can teach us compassion and it can teach us about the kind of person we want to be going forward. If you lose that friendship in the process, while that sucks, we learn. It doesn't make us bad. We now have data and tools to not do it again. It may or may not be mendable. Feel free to try—but 100%, learn.

And possibly my favorite Brene quote on shame, "What we don't need in the midst of struggle is shame for being human." I mean, come on!! Preach, Brene!

This is where we can pile all the things in our life that we can't control—my disability. Getting laid off from a job—under circumstances you didn't cause and don't control. Being sexually assaulted. Being gay. Being black or white or any other color. There is no shame in who God made us to be. And there is no shame in circumstances that are beyond our control.

We are humans having a human experience. Sometimes things go wrong. Sometimes we DO wrong. Sometimes we get hit out of left field by things we'd rather not experience or have to live through. Being human and having a human experience is not anything that holds space for shaming ourselves. You wouldn't let a friend do it, so don't do it to yourself.

Let's make a pact—I'll hop off the shame bus, if you will. From now on, I shine my light on "Bob," and I will see it for what it is. I will do what I can to make amends when necessary, and I will learn and do better.

Finally, repeat after me. "Because I do wrong, doesn't make me wrong. I am worthy of love and forgiveness."

Chapter 11:
Discrimination

I am not a victim.

There are people who may have tried—and may try again—to *victimize or dehumanize* me through acts of discrimination, but I will never BE a victim. It is MY choice—not theirs—as to whether I become a victim or whether I live as a human being, entitled to take up the same space as them.

Nope, not a victim. What I AM is a disabled, 47-year-old, *human* woman living in America. In a number of circles, that is three strikes against me—Disabled. Woman. Close to 50 years old. But what I know to be true is this. I am a woman of faith and I believe my creator intentionally made me as a woman, as a disabled person (I know, we can have a WHOLE debate about that sometime, but that's what I believe), and I believe he's kept me on this Earth for 47 years, with no signs of calling me home just yet. And I've had some close calls.

So, if what I've just said is true, then I am clearly here to be a specific person and to live a specific journey. If there is judgment or inequality that comes with that journey, I am prepared to deal with it.

Notice, I didn't say, "accept it." I didn't say, "live with it." I said, "deal with it." I have, and I will continue to. Because, I am not a victim, and I refuse to live or behave like one, regardless of how others see, treat or interact with me.

I want to be very clear of my intention in this chapter because it could be a triggering topic for some. There are a lot of people on this Earth who have been on the receiving end of discrimination for a plethora of reasons. Just being discriminated against is a violation of a person, and it is 100% not up to me to decide how a person who's stood in those shoes *should* handle it, deal with it or respond to it. Like so many other things in this life, that decision is up to each individual person. What I want to do in this chapter (which is frankly, my intent with all the chapters I write for this book) is to talk about my experience and how I choose to handle it, deal with it and respond to it. My way may not be your way, but what I can tell you is that I've found the way I've handled it to be empowering. Which is the exact opposite of what discrimination is intended to do. I've found it to be effective. And I want you to know that if you have been, are being, or will be discriminated against, it's not ok. I hope that you will choose (in the words of Michelle Obama), when they go low, to go high. Choose to empower *yourself* and not to let anyone take your power or your rights away from you.

I've talked about the power of a definition in other chapters, and I think that this is a chapter where a definition can be particularly effective. I know what discrimination is, and I'm sure you do, too, but when I read some definitions, it brought a new kind of understanding and clarity to this topic for me. Here is what I found in a Merriam-Webster about discrimination: "the practice of unfairly treating a person or group of people differently from other people or groups of people."

I also found this definition within a Wikipedia article that summed it up nicely for me: "discrimination is defined as wrongfully imposed disadvantageous treatment or consideration."

The first example I can think of where this became present in my life was kindergarten. Yaaaasssss, just five years in and I was faced with discrimination. Granted, I was beginning kindergarten in 1978, however, the public school in Ft. Worth, TX I was set to go to told my mom I'd have to join a special ed class. Because I couldn't stand or walk. That was all. I could speak, I could play, I could sit crisscross-applesauce, I could learn the alphabet, I could sing songs, I could make macaroni necklaces, I could count to 10 as quickly as any other 5-year-old. But, because I couldn't stand or walk, my mom was told I couldn't participate in a "regular," mainstream class.

Know what she did about it? She fought it. In 1978, she knew I did not deserve to be treated any differently than any other child simply because I couldn't stand or walk. While other mothers of incoming kindergartners were basking in the glow of their child's upcoming milestone, my mom had to make phone calls, and go to meetings and show up in administration offices just so her child could have the same experience as the other kids. She won, but it was a battle she shouldn't have had to fight to begin with.

Was that the last time she had to fight or advocate for me to join a regular, non-special-ed class? Nope. Because schools, at the time, lumped all disabled people, regardless of understanding individual function or capabilities, into a single, narrow, diminished category that could not coexist with "normal" kids.

This is a judgement that could have cost me DEARLY and changed the entire sequencing and outcome and quality of my life. If my potential had been judged purely on my ability to walk, I would have been cheated out of the appropriate education AND socialization for me. I might not have gone to college. I might not have earned a master's degree. I may not have led global teams of highly skilled professionals or become a speaker, a writer, or the host of TWO podcasts. I might not be writing this book.

This is also a judgement that could have cost the hundreds, or thousands of other kids who ended up "coexisting" with me in elementary, middle and high school for 13 years the benefit of being exposed to the crucial diversity of a person in a wheelchair and allowing it become normal for *them*. Their interactions with me may very well have affected how they went on to live their lives and interact with and potentially include disabled people in their work or in their lives because they went to school every day with a super-cool, super-smart chick in a wheelchair, and so they had the firsthand understanding that I was okay. That I was capable. That I could be a friend. That I could think and speak and be smart, and that I could lead them as the VP of the Key Club, the National Honor

Society AND the Honors Choir my senior year of high school (Take THAT, Ft. Worth elementary school who shall not be named!).

Discrimination manifests in a lot of different ways. If you look at the definition I gave earlier, it talked about the *treatment* of people in different groups or categories. It can be as overt as calling someone a derogatory name, using hate-speech, or denying someone a job because of their classification. And it can be as subtle as letting your kids just stare at someone in public instead of telling them to say, "hi," or those times when people spoke over my head to my mom or to my husband, asking questions like, "Does she want to sit inside or outside?" Thankfully, I've surrounded myself with people who *know* my ability to respond, and their answer has been something like, "I don't know, I guess you should ask her."

If you treat someone as "less-than" or deny them opportunities because they look different or fall into a category you aren't comfortable with, that's discrimination. If you've read the chapter on "Unemployment" already, you know that I was out of work for 10 months after leaving my last company. In that time, I interviewed for 53 jobs—going through SO MANY of them with 3-5 rounds of interviews. Do I *know* I didn't get any of them because of my 47-year-old, disabled woman status? No, not for sure. What I DO know is that I have crazy credentials and a breadth and depth to my experience that makes me unique. I have 20 years of experience. I had the numbers game on my side with the number of jobs I was interviewing for and that I was apparently doing well enough in to be invited back 2, 3, 4 or 5 times. When you have so much evidence in your favor that you are qualified, it's hard not to wonder if there was discrimination and bias at play because people wondered if I was going to need complicated, expensive accommodations (PS, I didn't), and the other top candidate didn't. Maybe, maybe not.

After 10 months, it caused me to question my very worth. Was I worth asking a couple extra questions about what accommodations I might need in an office? It appeared I was not. Discrimination causes the individual to feel undervalued, at best. And at worst—completely worthless. Discrimination alienates you from society. It makes you feel alone.

It makes you feel wrong. To combat the feeling of worthlessness and "wrongness," takes a resilient soul, and I have worked hard in my life to become just that—resilient. I've got the callouses to prove each time I've gotten back up and make no mistake—I'm scrappy!

So, I say again, I am not a victim, and I won't behave like one. What I did instead was, I put my work boots on, put a smile on my face and I built my own career where I've had just as much success AND where I have the honor of using my voice to impact others. I empowered *myself.* I realized I didn't need other people to empower me to go back to work. I could do that on my own, once again, proving what I was made of. And probably, why those other companies should have hired me! Their loss.

So here is the thing. While I am not a victim, and I refuse to let others victimize me through something like discrimination, what I don't believe in is combating hate or ignorance with more hate or ignorance. I take responsibility for *myself,* and for how I am perceived in the world. I work harder, I love harder, I forgive harder. I have fought and worked so hard to have the life I have and to be the intentional person I am, and I won't let a person who doesn't know (or care to find out) the badass I am and the person who makes judgements about me based on the chair I sit in all day dictate how I show up in this world. I know who I am and I am happy to share that truth with anyone who is paying attention. And if they're not—they may not be for me.

So, is it *my job* to educate that person about disability or about being a woman? No. It's my choice and I *choose* to be part of the solution. In fact, one of my core values is to live as a solution-oriented person, instead of a problem-oriented person. I identify with the solution—not with the problem. It's why I choose to advocate for the disabled community for things like equal experiences in air travel and for accessibility. By knowing who I am, by showing up intentionally as a person I am proud to be and who will have no regrets when my head hits the pillow at night, by loving and forgiving and educating where I can, I am not a victim. I'm empowered. No matter what job "they" won't give me. No matter what school I have to fight to go to. No matter how I am treated by the restaurant hostess or the store clerk, I am not a victim because I choose who I am and how I show up. How THEY show up? That's *their* responsibility, and I am trying to lead by example. They'll either learn or they won't.

The part of me who loves and forgives harder also knows that people fear what they don't know. If you haven't had a disabled person in your life, I get that some might not be comfortable with it. I do—I understand. Even though that knowledge stings a little, I understand (whether it's okay or not) that their discomfort may lead to fear that keeps a person from hiring me. I get it. I do. And in my advocacy work, I am working hard to encourage the people who build the world around us, to build it to be universally accessible. I am encouraging businesses and the media to put individuals with disabilities in our direct line of sight every day, so we can be seen and normalized and "interacted with" on the regular, so that those with no disabled person in their life can get comfortable with seeing us in the world, and thereby, interacting with us.

However. Here comes the tough love. I also challenge people to put on their big girl or big boy panties and I ask you, with all the love in my heart, to put yourself in situations on purpose where you *can become* comfortable with it. Just as I take responsibility for who I show up as in the world—we can all take responsibility for enlightening ourselves and creating opportunities for exposure to people who are different from us. Hire someone in a wheelchair, or with hearing impairments or visual impairments and watch the perspective and the different set of skills they bring to your company, making it stronger, better, and more competitive.

Businesses should ask themselves, what are the different perspectives and the different sets of life skills they bring—for me, because of my disability, I am a great problem-solver. I think outside the box. I have great empathy and compassion for people and that makes me a great leader of people. I am loyal, I am hard-working, dedicated, and resilient.

Invite someone from church or work or school—anywhere—who doesn't look like you out for coffee. This is not meant to be a chapter all about disability. Have people in your circle of different physical abilities, races, genders, sexual orientations. On purpose. Like I said before—discrimination can be directed toward any person who falls into a "category" you don't belong to.

Honestly—I believe solution number one to this problem is inclusion. If everyone in our lives looks like us—same gender, same race, same physical abilities, sexual orientation, same financial or professional status—we are missing out. Being around people who don't "look" like you gives new perspective. It gives empathy. It opens our eyes. If it doesn't occur naturally in our worlds, let's be intentional about making it happen. Diversify your inner circle.

I believe the other solution is visibility. By creating more intention in the media and in entertainment to positively represent and include ALL PEOPLE—again, all races, all genders and sexual orientations, all ages, all physical abilities—we can normalize the differences between us and thereby, lessen the opposition, the fear or the discomfort we may feel when someone who is not like us comes in to our place of business, or applies to interview for a job with us.

I think the last thing I have to say about the idea of discrimination is that the other bit *I control* in the situation is how I respond to it. We may not be able to control what's happening, but we can ALWAYS control our response to what's happening. And the good news there is that this means that we can potentially control the outcome. Owning your response puts you back in the driver's seat. So often when these bad things happen, we feel out of control—this is one way to get it back. So, in these situations where I've experienced discrimination, I've responded with as much grace, gratitude, kindness, understanding and forgiveness as I can muster. Then, I put a smile on my face, and I empower myself to take another step, or to try something else, or to respond to the individual in a way that corrects, but doesn't shame them.

Here's the thing. I will be a disabled person for the rest of my life. FACT. I have choices about how I respond to that. Choice number one—I can sit at home all day, every day, feeling sorry for myself and watching daytime TV (nothin' but love for you, daytime TV!). Or, choice number two—I can be a disabled person, out in the world, where things may require more effort, take longer for me to do and be a little harder, and where people may judge or treat me unfairly, but I am HAPPY and living the life I want, instead of the life so many have underestimated on my behalf.

When you or someone you love is on the receiving end of this problem, I challenge you to decide who you want to be, and what example you want to set in difficult times. Do you want to be bitter, angry, play the blame-game and make everyone around you miserable, and cause people to run away from you instead of wanting so badly to stick their necks out and do all they can to help? Great. Do that.

For me, I'm choosing to control who I am, who I show up as, who I represent my own dang self as in this world, and how I respond when bad things happen or when people treat me unfairly. I choose to use my voice in a kind way, in an informative way, in a way that doesn't breed more hate and blame. But in a way that educates where I can and in a way that can perpetuate change because I showed up as (I hope) someone people want to know and learn from and see more of.

Let me be clear. I am in no way giving a pass to those who discriminate against others. There are so many reasons why someone might do that. The reasons could stem from ignorance, from laziness, from financial business decisions. Or it could come from more egregious places—hate or supremacy.

What I have learned in my life so far, however, is that I cannot control others. I CAN control myself. I can try to influence others by being the person I am and by being as good a "me" as I know how to be. I can be a constructive member of society. I can work to educate and advocate. But just as I refuse to be a victim, I refuse to stoop to the level of the person discriminating against me and fight back with hatefulness, shaming and blaming. That isn't who I am. The last thing the world needs in the face of something founded on either ignorance or hate, is more ignorance or hate.

I choose to treat that person how I would like to have been treated. With respect and dignity and kindness. And if that doesn't work, I believe from the bottom of my heart that "what goes around, comes around."

Chapter 12:
The Struggle to Become a Mom

Sometimes, things that suck, can be a blessing in disguise.

When I was 22, my neurologist confirmed what I pretty much already knew. I had all the correct equipment for having children biologically, but that to do so would be a bad idea. I know, normally you'd have this conversation with an OB/GYN, and I did, later, to verify what my neurologist had said (and he did agree), but my neurologist knew about the ins and outs of my condition and how my body would respond to a pregnancy.

My neuromuscular condition had caused significant atrophying to the muscles all over my body. In addition to not being able to walk, my arms are affected, my neck and my trunk muscles are affected. Everything. My respiratory function is less than normal, and I've heard stories about women with perfectly good respiratory function who lie awake at night in months seven, eight, and nine of their pregnancy, struggling to breathe. It would be a high-risk pregnancy. I'd would have had to be on bed rest for a long amount of time, which would cause my muscles to further atrophy, and then I might never regain that strength. And never mind the issue of a baby pressing on your bladder when you can't use the bathroom independently. I mean, yikes.

Then there was the baby to consider, of course. My condition is genetic. Would I pass it to the child? I wouldn't be able to do so much of what a baby needed—picking it up when it was crying, changing diapers, feeding, dressing. When it started walking, being able to grab its hand *before* the finger went into the electric outlet, and being able to snatch them up before they ran out into the busy street or parking lot. The list went on.

I will say, for full transparency, I have heard of other women with my same condition having babies since I went through my journey. I am happy for them, of course, but there is a lot I don't know about them. I don't know their medical status compared to mine. I don't know what their relationship with their partner is like. I don't know what their doctors advised them to do or not to do. All I know is what I was being told by doctors I trusted, the risks I was being presented with and how I felt.

I also knew that there are a lot of ways to create families, I was open to ALL possibilities, and somewhere deep inside, I knew the child who needed me—and who I needed—would find us the way they were meant to.

Don't get me wrong. The news of this sucked. While I was open and hopeful, being a young woman who wanted a life partner and wanted a family, it took some mind-work to wrap my brain around it. Going on dates and knowing one of the standard questions, "do you want kids," was coming—I knew my answer—that yes, I wanted kids very much, but that I couldn't have them biologically, but really wanted to adopt— would disqualify me from a lot of relationships. And, I still wasn't old enough to be entirely secure in my own skin and in my own existence to not feel the rejection deeply when that was a deal-breaker with a guy, or when after that conversation, I never heard from him again.

I had a lot of baggage (don't we ALL?!) that I have talked about in this book that, at the very center of that baggage, made me believe I wasn't good enough. Good enough for someone to be my friend, to hire me, to ask me out. To love me. Having to admit to a guy that yet another thing was "wrong" with me that would affect the hypothetical life we could have together. It sucked. And, I lived a lot of years feeling badly about that part of myself. I knew, logically, that I would (hopefully) find someone who was the right one for me—who would love me enough and be as open to the idea of alternate ways to become a parent as I was. But, when you're in the thick of it, living the suck, hoping for the happy ending you haven't found yet? Well, it's hard.

I found him in 2001. We met online, when online dating was just starting to become a thing, but everyone was still "in the closet" about it. That's a whole other story, but suffice it to say, we got married two years later, and about another two or three years after that, we started talking seriously about expanding our family. We decided at a dinner out one night that "We were officially trying."

What that meant was that I would begin researching every option known to man—seriously—to adopt. I talked to so many people. I talked to people about domestic adoption. I talked to people about foster-to-adopt. I talked to people at 97 different adoption agencies about adopting from every country on the planet. Okay, I exaggerate a smidge, but not much. Ethiopia, Mexico, Peru, China, Japan, Kazakhstan. On and on and on. I wanted to leave no stone unturned so that we could be put on the right path to THE child who was meant to be ours.

For the reasons I mentioned about my physical challenges with taking care of a baby, we had decided to adopt a child who was around four or five years old. And, I knew a fair amount about the emotional (and sometimes, physical) trauma a child of that age could have been subject to. I did so much research, made so many phone calls. But, China. We kept coming back to China. I felt drawn to it, and I'd found that the adoption agency that was THE BEST—the absolute experts at Chinese adoption, just happened to be based in Austin, where we lived. All signs were pointing to China…until they weren't. Or, were they?? But, I'm jumping ahead.

We went to an information night the agency offered. Got all the info, heard what the process was like, heard from some couples who had been through the experience. We were sold. Because of the age of the child we wanted, we left there *knowing* our daughter existed in China and was waiting for us—that was the urgency I felt. OMG, the heartstrings on that!

The next day (seriously, the next day—when I commit to a goal, kids, get out of my way!), I began filling out the application and doing all the things the adoption agency needed to be able to submit our application. I think I had it all submitted in something like five days, and that was only because we needed letters of reference. I was not playing around. At that point, I was a mom who needed to bring her child home.

I was in my office at work when the call came in. The voice on the other end of the phone said, "there is no easy way to say this, but they've refused your application based on your health condition." I didn't miss a beat—we knew going into it that my disability would be questioned, but it had never, not for one second, occurred to us that we would be outright denied.

I was used to navigating situations like this, "Okay, what is the appeals process?" I asked. And she said, "Unfortunately, there isn't one. They've made their decision, and these things are never overturned. I'm so sorry we can't help you."

We hung up. Wait. What? But my daughter is waiting for me. I started to cry. And I left work and went home and cried some more. And I called my mom, and we both cried. I couldn't imagine telling my husband that, once again, because of me, he wasn't going to get to be a dad. I couldn't breathe.

Then, something started to happen. I started to get angry. I thought to myself, "Wait a second. These people don't *know me*. All they know is what we were allowed to tell them in the fields of their application. They don't really know *me*, know what I've overcome. They don't know the life I've architected and the independence I live with and the skills and capabilities I have that will allow me to take care of this child. They don't know my heart and my soul."

I thought back to the information night and I remembered the woman who had run it. I'd felt a connection with her, and she was a real-life human-being who had met us and seen our will to adopt and had heard our story. She wasn't just a voice on the phone or a person on the receiving end of our adoption application. I found her business card and I fired off an email to her explaining what had happened, and basically begged her to help us. Within five minutes, I had an email back from her that said, "It ain't over 'till the fat lady sings. Let me see what I can do."

Before I knew it, we had a plan. I was to put together a packet of information with more letters of recommendation—I got letters from friends, from my doctors, from my employers. I had a video tape (yes, this was pre-DVD and YouTube) of me singing on national television. I put everything we could think of into a packet that would convince the government of China that I was "fit." She also enlisted the help of the adoption agency owner who saw my packet and jumped into action for us. She made phone calls, she called in favors—for us. For real, there are people living on this planet who truly are angels.

It took a little time, but eventually, as I was sitting in my same office where I'd gotten the call that made me cry—I got the email that made me cry. It was a picture of my daughter. It was her medical record. It was commentary about how she loved to sing and share food. I was smitten. They said to take the weekend to think about it, but I called my husband, sent him the info, and we had our very firm "YES" back to them in 10 minutes.

It was another six months after that before we could get on a plane to bring her home, and it was agonizing. She turned five during those months, and I couldn't be with her. We had a bit more back and forth that made us wonder if this miracle would happen after all (by that, I mean they changed their minds more than once), and I honestly didn't quite believe it until we were on a plane, headed for Beijing. I felt every bit the pregnant woman who was two months overdue. But it was happening. We were going to bring her home.

That is not all that needed to happen, however. Have you ever tried going to China in a wheelchair? OMG. So much to figure out. This country in not like the United States—it (and its architecture) is THOUSANDS of years old, and there is no ADA there. One of the plusses, however, of working with this adoption agency was that they could assign us a personal guide who lived in China to be with us 24/7. We had to be there for two weeks, and go to three different cities to make it all happen.

We worked for *months* beforehand with their Chinese staff to check out how transportation was going to work. There were no cars we could use that had wheelchair ramps, so they arranged for minivans (that I think were left over from 1960) and I had to be lifted in and out of them and my manual wheelchair had to be folded up and put it in the back of the van.

We needed people to assess how accessible each hotel we would stay in would be—like, down to the layout and size of the bathrooms in the hotels. We had to fly to each of the cities we'd be going to, so we had to look into whether there was a normal jetway on and off the planes or if we'd have to navigate down stairs to exit the planes. Did the various hotels have elevators or just stairs? Between the transportation situation and ALL THE STAIRS we knew we'd encounter everywhere we'd be going, I couldn't take my electric wheelchair. It had to be a manual wheelchair that folded up, which honestly, took away my remaining physical independence for the two weeks we spent there.

While we were there, we saw so many amazing things, (The Great Wall, The Forbidden City, Tiananmen Square) but it was hard. AND it was also magical. We were novelties in China. My parents came with us, and my mom and I were both blonde. We were Americans, AND I was in a wheelchair. Somewhere, over in China, there are A LOT of phones and cameras with photos of us on them.

Then, in our second city, Zhengzhou, we met her. They'd set up a time to bring her to our hotel. All I could think about was how scary this had to be for her. She was five and she *knew* what was happening. To be brought to a hotel and handed over to strangers, who didn't speak your language and who were going to take you across the ocean, away from everything you knew? I wanted to cry for her, but I also wanted so badly to love her and give her a good life and be the mother she deserved.

We waited impatiently in our hotel room, and finally, the phone rang. They were there. We took the longest elevator ride ever down to the lobby, and as the elevator doors opened, my breath caught. I saw her instantly, sitting on the floor, leaning her back against a chair, her knees pulled up to her chin, hair in ponytails, one small bag beside her. It was like seeing a celebrity for the first time. I knew her, but I didn't *know* her.

Our guide had taught me to say, "I'm your mommy" in Mandarin. As we approached, she stood up, and she happened to put her hand on my arm. I said the words that had been taught to me, and she giggled—apparently, my pronunciation left something to be desired. But within five or 10 minutes, she was sitting on my lap, and coloring with my husband on a coffee table.

There were some officials there, watching, and having us sign paperwork. They said that normally they'd check in and have another visit, but that they were so happy with what they were seeing, they wanted to make it official for us that day. We spent the rest of the day visiting different offices and notaries. It was the happiest day of my life. I didn't know you could love—SO much.

Today, she is 20 years old and going to college. She is one of the bravest people I've ever met, and I love her in a way I never understood until I was a mother. Her happiness is my happiness. Her sadness is my sadness, and I want every good thing possible for her. She has no idea how incredible she is and I am waiting for the day when she will realize it. She's so special, and I can't imagine being a mother to anyone else. I can't imagine loving anyone more, even if they came from my body. *She* came from my heart. She completed our family. She made us parents. I will be forever grateful to China for seeing that we could give her a good life and for entrusting her to us.

This whole journey, from deciding to pursue adoption, to meeting our daughter in the lobby of our hotel in China took about a year and half. For so many women who have had fertility struggles, or worked with surrogates or who also adopted, that may be small potatoes. I've spoken to women who deal with infertility or other issues and their journey have taken five, or eight, or ten years. It's agonizing.

The emotional struggle is awful. It comes down to such a basic function of what a female body should be able to do. When your body fails you—when you can't do what you were built to do, and one of the biggest things that sets you apart from the opposite sex, I've felt the shame. It made me feel wrong and inferior and unwanted and rejected.

I know all the feels. I *don't* pretend to know your journey, but I do know the struggle.

It's hard. It's lonely. It's disappointment after disappointment. You sometimes feel like no one has ever failed so badly or been so alone in their troubles.

But here is the thing. My struggles to become a mother led me to *this* child. I don't take that lightly. I believe that my struggle to become a mother serves to underscore how much I was meant to be *her* mother. She is the one who was ultimately granted to us. After fighting and justifying and begging and praying, it was her. I will be the first to tell you that I have not been a perfect mother, but I have been pretty darn good. I've loved her and cheered for her. I've grounded her and I've bought her her first lipstick. Perfect, no—but I believe, SO meant to be.

Life is a journey full of paths to very specific destinations that manifest at the end of those long, hard roads. This road could have ended very differently. It could have ended with no child, which would have been devastating, but I would hope that it would be because I was needed elsewhere. I would hope I'd be able to see the alternate path life was taking me on and give it everything I had. Life is meant to be enjoyed—not regretted. Things don't always turn out the way we'd planned. But sometimes they turn out better. This was one of those times. My inability to have children biologically WAS a blessing in disguise, and I can see that now. The hurt and the anguish was for a reason. It guided me toward this little soul who I believe I was destined for (though, she might have disagreed those days when I grounded her.).

If you are struggling to have children—whatever the cause—I am so, very sorry. I know the heartbreak and the desire and the disappointment. I know the feeling of believing you are denying your spouse. I know the self-esteem that suffers. It is so hard—when all you want to do is love? It seems so wrong not to be able to do it.

I was open to exploring the other ways families are made, and honestly—there are so many possibilities. If you can put the hurt aside, and again, decide you are not a victim and allow yourself to be open to ALL the possibilities, I believe the right one will present itself.

That said, take your time. Do your research. I've learned so much over the years, and I believe whole-heartedly in the counsel I am about to give.

If, for example, you choose to adopt an older child like we did, understand their history and special needs and make sure you are prepared to address them. It is so easy to get caught-up and romanticize the act of creating a family (and it is beautiful, don't get me wrong), but so many of these kids have been hurt in ways we could never understand. None of that was their fault, and it will ultimately be up to you to get them through it.

Any child we have—even a biological child—can be born with any number of challenges we didn't count on. If you are choosing to create your family through adoption, make sure you understand the challenges THIS child comes with and be prepared to help them through it. That is your job as a parent. Don't rush to make a choice out of excitement. Be thorough and don't let your ego get in the way of realizing you may need to learn some things about how to best parent THIS child. Make sure you are the right one to do it. If you're not, there is NO shame in that, either. If you know you're not equipped and can't get equipped. That's brave. And it gives the child a chance to find their right home and receive their best shot.

If not adoption, maybe surrogacy, or fostering, or donor eggs...ad infinitum. So. Many. Possibilities. So much of being a parent is being open to your child, who they are and what they need. Start early. Be open in your pursuit of them—be as open as possible, and I do believe solutions present themselves.

And, if this journey is not meant for you? I'm sorry. There is still life to live and love to be given and reciprocated and experiences to have. All is not lost, even though it might feel like it for a minute. Surrender. Surrender to what you *are* meant for and what you are called to do in this life. There are other paths, and it's ok if you don't know what yours is yet. You will find it—or maybe, it will find you. And if you let it, I know that alternate path can lead to joy.

Chapter 13:
Rejection

You might be expecting me to begin this chapter with alllllllll the ways I've been rejected by the world. Surprise—I want to begin by talking about how I've rejected *myself*. We'll talk about the world in a minute.

I had a therapist for a short time in college—I remember sitting in her office one day, and she had asked me to list all the things I liked about myself. Know what I said? "I'm nice to animals." That was all I could come up with. We had a little work to do.

Why is it so hard, sometimes (or all the time), for us to give ourselves credit for being wonderful? For me—for most of my life, in addition to having a hard time believing I was anything special, I thought it was—I don't know—*bad manners* or something to admit I might have done something great or *been* anything to write home about. I believed it was bragging, if I said or thought anything positive about myself, and bragging was bad.

What if I heard someone else pat themselves on the back? Well, that was fine, of course! But the rules were different for them, weren't they? C'mon! If you are anything like me, you get it. Someone else can be great, but heaven forbid we believe it of ourselves. Anyone?? Yes, I see you.

What *is* that? I'm not going to lie—I still get squishy on the subject when I turn the lens on myself. I know in my rational brain that it's completely illogical. I also know what a widespread commonality it is between so many women.

It occurs to me that if we have poor self-esteem or poor self-confidence, what that *really is,* is our own rejection of ourselves. I'm sure there are much better, more scientific ways to look at it, but it helps me to look at it that way. Rejection is a triggering word—no one wants to be rejected. And if you turn the tables on yourself and recognize that what you are actually doing when you can't or refuse to see your worth—is rejecting yourself. Sit with that for a minute.

For me, the strongest antidote to my own rejection is goals. When I was working on my singing career, I had to step out of my head and believe I could carry a tune. When I was working on my master's degree, I had to, somewhere inside me, believe I deserved to be sitting in those classes. Three years ago, when I lost my job, and went through 10 months of fruitless job hunting, (on the heels of SO MUCH *external* rejection—remember those 53 jobs I interviewed for but didn't get?) and started working to employ myself and build a business as a speaker, a podcast host, a coach and a writer, I had to wake up every day and tell myself to stop being a bully and to believe I was good enough to complete the next step.

By working toward my goals, I've built up some muscle around believing I am capable, talented, worth listening to. Here's the deal, though—goal or no goal, we all go through life collecting all kinds of evidence (whether we choose to acknowledge the evidence or not) that we are good. We have friends we are good to. We have people who seek us out to spend time or to talk or seek our counsel. We have families we love and who love us. We have individual strengths and talents. We pay our bills. Some of us are great at telling jokes. Some of us are good listeners. We hold doors open for each other. Some of us make a mean pot of chili or spaghetti. Some of us read to children and use fun voices. Some of us smile at each other in the grocery store. Some of us are good moms. Some of us are good businesspeople (some of us do both!). Some of us would give the shirt off our backs to another person who needs it. We buy cookies from Girl Scouts (come on—that's ALL of us!). Some of us are really nice to animals. Sorry, couldn't resist.

The good things we do during our lifetime—the talents we have, our accomplishments, the kindnesses—those things exist whether we choose to see them or not. If you are reading this book—you're one of my "people," and I only hang with awesome people. So, I hereby declare you—awesome. Take an unencumbered inventory of your life today— the people in it, the way you spend your time, your work, your school, the small (or big) acts of kindness, the goals you've accomplished. That's your evidence. Write it down on paper so you can see all of it. When you see it written down, you can't disparage it. So, let's stop rejecting ourselves. Promise?

But what about external rejection, though? It feels like we have *some* control over our rejection of ourselves—and we *will*. Remember our promise?

When we are rejected by someone else—that can almost even inform our rejection of ourselves. Don't do it, friends. I'm not letting you break our promise! But let's discuss it.

Rejection sucks. It can eat at the core of our being. After all, the message we are receiving is that we are not wanted, or not valued, or not good enough. Right? Or is it? Those might be the messages we're receiving, but have they been decoded the right way? I suspect not.

Dating is an obvious and—OMG—SUCH a universally sucky thing. Try dating in a wheelchair, y'all—super-fun!

I didn't date much until my mid-late twenties. Let's just rip that band-aid right off. When I was in high school, there was one boy—ever— interested in me. Unfortunately, I didn't feel the same—and can I just say, I've heard it said that because of my disability, I should just be glad to have anyone who showed me interest. Check, please! Don't get me wrong—this guy was a perfectly nice, funny, cute guy—he just wasn't for me. *And that was allowed!* Despite my wheelchair status and what some said I should be "grateful" for, I was still allowed to have likes and dislikes and preferences and chemistry. Or, a lack of chemistry with people.

I had a bunch of crushes in high school. A bunch. The crushes were never returned. I saw my friends date and I wanted to be part of that club, but besides high-school-age boys, for the most part, not being mature enough or secure enough to date the girl in the wheelchair, I couldn't get around. I couldn't get in and out of cars, so a guy couldn't come over and pick me up for a date. And I was the first to object to my parents dropping me off for a date. Talk about social suicide! (Don't worry, Mom and Dad—your granddaughter would have said the very same about me if she'd had the same problem. Your parents are just embarrassing when you're in high school.)

So, I spent a lot of Friday and Saturday nights alone, feeling sad and lonely and wishing it could be different (see chapter on loneliness!). I didn't feel particularly pretty in high school. I felt awkward, I felt over-weight, and I was pretty shy. Not a strong combo to attract the interests of the young gentlemen.

Then there was college. And the "freshman 15" (maybe 25, in my case). And the wheelchair. And the roommate who looked like a supermodel who every boy on campus wanted to date. I got used to the phone never being for me. Until it was. There were actually *three* guys in college (in the whole entire four years) who showed interest in me—but again, I didn't feel the same. So, I sabotaged them. And then I wondered what in the hell I'd done when I was lonely and second guessing if maybe I should actually have just been grateful and said, "please and thank you." I wondered if anyone would ever come along where the feeling was mutual.

Again, I had TONS of crushes. TONS. Never returned. Ever. I'd come out of my shell in college, and despite some extra weight and the wheel-chair—still had transportation issues—I'd become kind of ridiculously fun to hang out with. I had a lot of male friends, but none of them ever showed any romantic interest (in me—LOADS OF THEM showed interest in my roommate). It sucked. I focused on being a fun friend and that had to do. But I was hopeful.

And finally—adulthood. I graduated college, still in a wheelchair (dang chair!), still overweight, still rejected by all the men. I had an apartment, a job, a service dog named Jenny, (who had no business being a service dog, but I loved her) and full control of the television.

I had been rejected a lot in my lifetime. But then, as you now know from a previous chapter, I made a decision to work on my health and losing weight and started feeling a little more attractive. And guess what I found? This was *just before* online dating began, and there was this commercial on TV at night for "The People Store."

I wish I were kidding. The only redeeming quality it had was that it was free. And all I know is—I wanted a boyfriend. This felt like a way for me to take control. You could call in, get a PIN to a mailbox, and leave a message about yourself—and then people could leave you messages. I'm pretty sure a few of the messages I got were from serial killers, but I went out with one or two of them whose messages "sounded" more normal. It didn't go anywhere. I still didn't get any second dates, but it put me out there, which was good training for—online dating (queue dramatic music).

It was circa 1999—Match.com was *just* coming on the scene. People were beginning to date online, but most were still in the closet about it—the stigma attached to it was akin to answering personal ads back in the day, and it felt kind of desperate (to be clear, that's how it felt back then because it was so new. I know that today, it's hard to find someone who *hasn't* dated online and it's perfectly acceptable—back then, less so). But my boss at the time, who was successful and beautiful and had it all together, told me she was doing it and that I should give it a try. So, I did. For six months—it was awful. Most of the people who got past the mention in my profile that I was in a wheelchair seemed to be gentlemen who had never been out of their houses in the daylight or ever spoken to a woman before.

There were countless guys who glossed over the part of my profile that mentioned my wheelchair (I mentioned it, because I was so tired of the disappointment. I figured I'd be open and honest—no surprises, no disappointment, right? Meh.). Oh, the ghosting when they found out. Once again, rejected and *wrong*.

Yes, dating sucked. When you are looking for someone to want you in every way possible—emotionally, socially, physically, intellectually—for the long haul, and no one does, it plays a lot of games with your self-esteem and your sense of worth. I wish I could say I was evolved enough back then to look, *then* at that lack of self-esteem and my sense of worth as my own self-perpetuating my rejection of myself, but I wasn't. I was sad. I was lonely. I hated my wheelchair.

If you are single and dating and your dating circumstances are wreaking havoc with YOUR self-esteem? Do as I say, not as I did. What I NOW know is that you only need one person. And to get to that person, you have to kiss a lot of frogs. That's just how it works. If you didn't have to kiss the frogs, you'd marry the first person you ever dated. Think back to the first person you ever dated. Yikes. Like the sentiment from the Garth Brooks song sometimes we have to thank God for the prayers he didn't answer because there was something we didn't know to ask for that would be better. If you are not for someone—then, really, are they for you? Do you *want* to be for them if they aren't all-in? If they don't think you're the best thing since a Snickers bar, do you want them?? It sucks. I get it. But if they are letting you go—do you really want them? Or do you want to be grateful to them for releasing you so you can either kiss the next frog, OR maybe meet your *actual* person? I say—be grateful. It's okay to be hurt. It's okay to feel duped, or deceived. It's even okay to feel rejected. But please, PLEASE, don't let that one person who you *just weren't right for,* and by extension, wasn't right for you—color what you know to be true about yourself. Remember all that evidence you gathered about who you are and who you have been in this world that makes you kind of awesome. That evidence is so much more significant than the person (who probably picks their nose in private) who did you the favor of moving on.

I wasn't for a lot of people. But that didn't mean I wasn't great. If you're great, you're great, and just because someone else doesn't see it or choose it, doesn't make it any less true. I see that now. I see my good qualities; I see what I bring to this world. I spent far too much time in my own life feeling unworthy, feeling ugly, feeling unwanted and feeling *wrong.* I felt like no one would ever choose me. What a waste of time.

And then, I met Michael. Michael was my last match on Match.com. I was about to throw in the towel there when I got another email. There was something different about it. It was sweeter and more genuine than the other emails I'd gotten. I took a few days to write him back, but when I did, and when we met for dinner, and sat talking for three hours, and he actually called the next day to say what a good time he'd had, and when he told me on our third date that he was falling in love with me (can I just tell you—that scared the ever-loving poo out of me!), I slowly began to believe this might be the person the world had in store for me—the one I had to kiss frogs and experience disappointment and hurt and rejection to eventually get to. 20 years later, he is still my person.

Trust. Anything we want to accomplish or attain in life requires that we trust the process. The process of kissing all the frogs, and having our self-worth challenged and our ability to keep going—it's a process. Trust it and know it is leading you to where you are supposed to be. Trust, and do not let ANYONE convince you along the way that you are not worthy and that is why you haven't reached the finish line yet. You may not have found your person or reached that finish line because better, different things or people are coming. Trust that and let it excite you. The excitement of what comes next can take some of the sting away that inevitably comes with rejection.

Rejection is part of life. We may be rejected by friends, by employers, by partners, by family. Trust what you KNOW to be true about yourself. Does it mean you won't make mistakes and that you won't be the one to sabotage something?

No.

You very well might—I sure did. Mistakes are also part of life. But what I *am* saying is that rejection is a standard part of this little life-contract we all have. It's part of the terms. It's part of the trade-off for all the amazingness we will ALL be recipients of.

And, if you can accept that—that rejection is part of life, and is NOT in *any way* defining of you, your character or your worth, it will help put you in a mindset to know exactly what you ARE worth and what you are deserving of, so you can hold on to that. Don't settle for less than you deserve. Rejection *tries* to tell us we suck—we don't.

Also—learn from rejection. Like everything else, I think it has something to teach us. Whether it's what we DO want, or who we want to be, or how we want to conduct ourselves going forward, we can take from it what serves us.

Just remember, we are having a human experience, and they were not for us. We deserve better. Trust. Be patient. You may have had to live this rejection so that something spectacular could show up, and so that you would appreciate the absolute gift it is when it arrives.

Chapter 14:
Comparison

I am fascinated by other people's bodies. Fascinated. It makes sense to me that with my own limitations, I'd be interested in what other people's bodies are capable of, and oh my goodness. Am I ever! I promise, I am not a creeper, but I watch people. Every day—I watch and I wonder, "What would that feel like, though?"

If someone crosses their legs, or raises their arms over their heads to stretch. I watch a person's calf muscles flex when they step up on a curb or climb stairs. I watch people vacuum, pushing and pulling the heavy thing over the carpet. I watch people sit on the sofa in our living room. Do you know that the only piece of furniture in my home I've ever sat on is my bed? I go from my wheelchair, to the toilet (sorry, but c'mon…), to bed. And I do that in reverse every morning. I've never sat on the sofa, or on one of our kitchen table chairs. Or the floor. If you ever come over for dinner—my sincere hopes that our furniture is comfortable!

I watch people sit on the passenger seat of my car, and I wonder if it's comfortable. I watch people stand at a stove, stirring a pot and I wonder if their arm gets tired. I watch someone sit in someone else's lap. I watch people embrace—I have people who hug me, but I can't hug back, and I wonder how it would feel to do the arm-wrapping.

I am not saying these things for sympathy. I SO am not; I hope you know me well enough by now. I am not feeling sorry for myself when I make these comparisons—I just wonder. I'm so intrigued by what other people's bodies whose muscles aren't atrophied, as mine are, can do. It's SO cool! The reaching, the stretching, the lifting, the standing, the climbing, the carrying. It amazes me and I wonder what it's like.

To reach up and scratch the top of my head when it's itching. To reach out and shake someone else's hand instead of opening my hand, smiling and willing them with my Jedi knight telepathy to reach out and shake MY hand…

These are everyday things I notice—I look at my body, and I look at "their" body, and I wonder. Every day, I wonder what it would feel like to NOT feel like you have 50-pound weights strapped to your arms that you can never unstrap, and I wonder, "Are that person over there's arms as effortless for them to pick up as I imagine they must be, or does it take effort?"

Then, there are more extreme examples—I LOVE—LOOOOOVE watching people do truly exceptional things with their bodies—Olympic gymnasts (OMG, Simone Biles, though???), aerial performers, ice-skaters (I once saw ice-skating aerial performers on a cruise ship—mind blown!), runners, divers (I'm sorry, but I *genuinely* don't understand how a diver's body does what it does—someone, explain to me how, in mid-air, while falling, you twist and turn and flip with that much intention, precision and control. HOW?? Not a rhetorical question—I really want someone to explain.), swimmers. It all boggles my mind, and I could watch it 24/7.

I always say that when I am a big enough name to have my own conference, I WILL have physical performers—dancers or acrobats—maybe Cirque du Soleil—or something to pay homage to what the human body, with the right conditioning, can actually do. Who's coming??

So yes. Comparison—I've spent my entire life comparing my body and my physical capabilities to other people's. And even though I am fascinated by it and don't say these things for pity, I also wonder—do people who don't have physical limitations put on their bodies appreciate their ability to walk up stairs, and raise their hand, and scratch their head? These things that look so easy for everyone else.

Comparison is not just reserved for our bodies, though. We compare our skills and professional success to others. We compare our parenting to others. We compare our finances to others. We compare the number of friends we have with others. We compare our cars, our kids, our homes, our spouses and partners, our connections.

I'm sitting here wondering—what do we get from comparison? Why do we do it? Here's how I see it. I see three categories of comparison. Sometimes comparison can be *interesting*, like my fascination with what a body does day-in-and-day-out with what seems like no effort at all, and in noticing and appreciating our differences. Comparison can also be *destructive*, though—when we compare our lack of perfection to someone else's "seeming" perfection (because truly, there is no such thing) and we abuse ourselves for it. AND comparison can be a *driver*—when we have a role model or a competition we are participating in (maybe that's what drives Simone Biles to such physical excellence). Someone else's excellence, if used positively and constructively, can drive our own excellence.

I've talked already in some detail about the *interesting* dimension of comparison. There is comparison that brings us joy. The way I am fascinated by the human body and by watching things flex and stretch and move with ease. Athletes and dancers bring me so much joy when I watch them. I think I have a heightened sense of appreciation for physical greatness because of what my body won't do.

Other things that might fall into this category are when you are making a big purchase and you're comparing features and prices and quality. Maybe when you're making a big decision—where to work, where to go to school, where to vacation, which doctor to see, even. This is all productive, constructive comparison—low emotion. Just comparison for information's sake.

I'm making a guess here, but I would venture to say that the most common "kind" of comparison is the destructive kind. This is the sucky side of comparison. It's so easy to fall into. When we compare, our insecurities can flare and that leads to shame and unworthiness and things like imposter syndrome.

I talked in the chapter on vanity about how I drove myself to some very destructive behaviors trying to "live up to" the world's ideal of what I thought it was telling me a woman should look like. So unhealthy. I told you—I made myself sick, and unhappy—and didn't even get any closer to the perfection I *thought* so many other women had. And I know about a bajillion other women who've also done it. I compared myself to the constant images online, in movies, on TV, in magazines—AND to top it off—I almost never see individuals in wheelchairs (people who look like me) in my direct line of sight. I wanted to be pretty. And what I thought the world thought was pretty was what I saw on TV, in movies, in magazines. And that was *not* how I looked.

In time, after comparing myself to something that doesn't even *really* exist (hello, airbrushing!) and making that my standard, my sense of worth plummeted, and my insecurity skyrocketed and I was terribly unhappy. I spent WAY too much time thinking about it and plotting how I could make *that* unrealistic reality come true. Fortunately, I've slowed my roll on making these comparisons and I have a much healthier mindset about perfectionism. Sucky, sucky form of comparison.

But there are other ways I've compared myself to others that have *also* been destructive. I've made unhealthy comparisons to my friends lives, to other parents, to other people I don't even know who seem to have success in areas where I don't. It's so bad! It takes your entire self-worth and your life (YOUR LIFE, Y'ALL!!), the thing you get out of bed every day and do., and makes it not good enough. That hurts my heart—I've done it. Let's be real—I *still* do it, but now, I also can catch myself when I do it and talk some sense into myself. This life—the one I have—that's MY journey, and I make it what it is. Their life—over there, the one my friend or neighbor or coworker are living, that's their journey. AND guaran-damn-teed there are things about their journey I don't know about that might not be as pretty as what I see on Facebook.

I've referenced imposter syndrome before, but "I.S." sits squarely at the center of comparison. Imposter Syndrome has become a huge buzzword in the personal and professional development space over the last year or two, and it's been eye-opening for me to talk to so many other women and to see how prevalent it is or has become (or maybe it's always been there and we've only just given a name to it). This kind of comparison—and comparison is what it is, make no mistake—is its own pandemic. Sucky! Women all over—women (and men) who I would have never expected, who seem so polished and accomplished, admit to imposter syndrome. The whole enchilada—the whole "who am I to…" Or "if they only knew what a fake I am…" or "I don't belong here." These incredible people I know and look up to are comparing themselves to other people who may not believe they belong either. What the what?? Know why? Because insecurity is a perfectly normal human emotion.

I've had the most gigantic case of Imposter Syndrome as I've built my career as a speaker, a writer, a coach and a podcast host. I'd watch the big dogs—Tony Robbins, Mel Robbins, Marie Forleo, Gabby Bernstein, and so on. In some ways, it's been helpful. When you are building something, you have no idea in heck how to build, you have to have some models. You need mentors and people to watch who can give you clues about how it's done. BUT. When you're comparing yourself to SUCH big names, again, the insecurity, you guys. I've had so many thoughts. So many feels. So much panic.

"I don't have as much to say as them."

"I can't possibly have the impact they've had."

"Who am I to try to step into the same space as them and do it as good or better?"

"Why on earth would anyone listen to me?"

"What makes me think I could do anything close to what they do?"

The answer to all those questions and the counter to the toxic thoughts—"because, I am me." I am NOT Tony Robbins, or Mel Robbins. I am me. I have nothing more than my own unique set of stories and thoughts and ideas and perspectives, JUST LIKE MEL. And maybe, that's good enough. I'll be Mindy Henderson and I'll see what I can do with that.

Don't get me wrong. I'm not done with imposter syndrome yet. I still wake up and have these toxic thoughts. Sometimes, rationalizing that "being Mindy Henderson" is my unique differentiator feels soooooo insufficient. But on the days when I can remember that, that is who I am and that is what I have to work with, the rest of it is about showing up and staying consistent and doing the work and improving over time. That's when the imposter syndrome subsides.

Action. It's the doing it anyway, the action and the forward movement and the taking another step, *despite* what my brain is telling me that puts imposter syndrome in its place. And, you know what? If you do that enough times—take action and keep moving forward and taking the next step, even when you don't fully believe you're good enough, that is how you start to believe you're good enough. Or how you BECOME good enough, because you keep going and keep practicing the skill. The proof is in the pudding, so to speak. And if I can keep my eye on the ball and keep working toward what I want—remain flexible and try something else when something isn't working, and just not quit, my brain will begin to believe that maybe I can stand with the big dogs. Every day, I see a little more possibility, and a little less imposter. Can I tell you what a good feeling that is??

So, the final category I named earlier is when we can use comparison as a driver in our lives. When I was working in high-tech, at the last company I worked for, I began as a Software Implementation Project Manager. After a couple years, I noticed that my coworkers—people who'd started around the same time as me, or after me, were being promoted to Senior Implementation Project Manager. Yet, I was beginning to feel stuck where I was. I felt unacknowledged and under appreciated. It started as an unpleasant and somewhat toxic comparison, because it just made me feel bad about myself.

Then, I experienced a couple of fortunate occurrences. The first was when I raised my hand to take on a difficult account that needed a dedicated Project Manager and some TLC. I was granted the account, which meant I would get transferred to a different manager. She was SUCH a blessing! I'm not sure what had been holding me back from promotions prior to this, but she was so welcoming and she showed a ton of excitement for the fact that (even if I didn't have the senior title) I had some seniority and her team was all relatively new. I fell into a mentorship role on her team with the other project managers, which gave me SO much confidence. AND THEN, our leadership team announced they were opening Team Lead spots for each of the implementation managers.

Having someone believe in you can make ALL the difference in our confidence—remember that. If you are a manager of people—it is your job to believe in them and to help them to be successful. And if you can't, it's your job to "re-home" them. To find somewhere they CAN be successful, or mutually agree to part ways.

All I needed from her was some affirming language and to see her believe in me and ask me to mentor a couple people and I had my ambition back. I decided to go for the Team Lead position, and I got it! I got the spot, working for my current manager, now as the Lead on her team. Turns out, Senior Implementation Project Manager wasn't my journey. My journey was to blow past it and take a Lead spot.

But wait, there's more! Then, our VP announced a month later that he needed to hire another manager. I talked to my current manager and she encouraged me to go for it. So, I threw my name in the hat. I was discouraged to have our VP tell me he would not be hiring from within. He wanted "fresh eyes" and would be hiring externally, but he told me it would be good practice for me to go through the interview process and to apply anyway.

I gave it to them with both barrels, my friends. I interviewed so hard, I can't even tell you. And, I am proud to say, I convinced that VP to hire me. What the what?? Best. Feeling. Ever. To this day, it is one of my proudest moments in my professional career. He actually decided to hire me AND an external person. Seriously—don't take no for an answer. Believe and go for it. Try harder and show up better than you ever have before!

So, to recap, not meant to be a Senior Implementation Project Manager. Nope. I went from Project Manager, to Lead, and a month or six weeks later, to Manager.

Here is what I think. Again, some comparison is for interest or information's sake. No emotion necessary. Perfectly healthy.

But there is sort of a tricky relationship between comparison that is destructive and comparison that is a driver. And, I think it's *possible* to turn destructive comparison into a driving force in your life. I think it boils down to insecurity and self-esteem, versus confidence and positivity.

The times in my life where comparison has been destructive, it's been because the thing I saw, admired and wanted, triggered some deep insecurity in me, and the insecurity was so deep and so ingrained in my mindset, and the emotion ran so high, that I couldn't put a plan together to get or to become the thing I wanted in a constructive, productive way. I tried shortcuts. I tried the same thing and failed at the same thing over and over again because I wanted it so desperately (and "desperate" is the operative word here). I believe in the Law of Attraction, and I believe that if the energy you're putting out there is desperate and charged in feelings of lack or failure, that is precisely what you will get. And I did. I got failure after failure that continued to feed my insecurity about what I believed was wrong with me, and the cycle of staying where I was continued.

BUT. The times when I have been able to remove the negative emotion from the equation, look at a goal in a more pragmatic way, create a plan, remain flexible and let the plan change when something wasn't working, and keep going? THAT is a confidence FEAST and the Law of Attraction was triggered by positivity and ambition and confidence rather than by desperation and hopelessness and lack.

I know it's easy to say and hard to do, and it is. But awareness is the first step—it's why you're reading this book, yes? It's because we want to take these things that can add so much "suck" to our lives and turn them on their ear. It's possible. If you are struggling under the weight of comparison right now, take a look at your mindset.

Are you stuck in a habit cycle of try-fail-repeat? Try something else. Are you looking at the thing you'd like to be or have from a place of lack and defeatism? Try making it a goal, and make a plan with steps you can execute on. Look for small steps and easy wins that will get you a little closer and boost your confidence. Action is power and if you take action, as you walk through those steps, your confidence builds, and you see that you can even fail at the plan you created, and still try something else and keep going. Confidence is a game-changer.

You don't know what comes along with the pretty picture of what someone else has, I promise. Keep that in mind. Behind closed doors, you have no idea what tradeoffs they may have made, or what they've suffered or given up. They are on their journey. You are on yours. Create what *you* want. Don't rehabilitate what you lack. See what the other person maybe has done and *admire* it. Don't look at it and let it be an indicator of how you've failed and need to be better. See the difference? By being positive, by getting into the right frame of mind to make change or to reach a goal, you can turn something so toxic and unhealthy into a powerful motivator.

Chapter 15:
Exclusion

When you live your life from a wheelchair, you spend a lot of time living in a world that is not entirely built for you. There are doors you can't get into. There are stairs you can't climb. There is public transportation you can't utilize. Because of this, I am a HUGE proponent of universal design. I learned about universal design when my husband and I built our current home. I wanted a house where every nook and cranny were accessible to me, but that didn't look like it had been built to be "accessible." *Anyone* could live in this house, wheelchair or not. I learned that there was a name for this, and I've spent a lot of time wondering since then, why this wouldn't just be the standard in the building of cities. If we are as progressive and *inclusive* a society as we claim to be, then why are there still places I can't go?

About 10 years ago, I broke my arm *because of* the lack of universal design—because of lack of accessibility. Because my physical abilities were excluded from the consideration of how and who could come and go from this building.

I had a job interview in downtown Austin. Now, it's true that downtown Austin has a lot of old, historic buildings that I suppose were grandfathered in and not deemed required to be made accessible if they were built prior to the Americans with Disabilities Act (ADA) that was passed in 1973. I don't know if this was one such building, but it definitely looked old.

I'd parked on the street about a block away. PS—the building had a parking garage, but I'm unable to reach all the way out of my window down to the machine to grab a ticket so the big arm will raise and let you into the garage to park. Can someone please fix that technology to remove the requirement to reach out and take a ticket so those of us who drive but have limited reach, can also participate in parking garage life? I digress…

So, there I was. I'd parked about a block away in some street parking. It was a sunny, warm day, so fortunately, that worked out fine and some fresh air before my interview wasn't a bad thing.

Then, I got to the building. It became really clear, really quickly that the building was going to be a challenge to get into. I found a few doors, but as soon as you opened them (or should I say, as soon as I stopped someone on the street and asked *them* to open the door, because, no door openers) there was either an immediate staircase up or an immediate staircase down. No floor to wander around on. Stairs up. Stairs down. Door after door, that was it.

My panic was growing because the clock was ticking and I didn't want to be late for this interview. I finally went around the building on the sidewalk that led into the garage. Another door, more stairs. Interview aside, I was actually kind of dying to get inside and see what the heck was inside this building besides stairs.

Fortunately, this time, there was a security guard. I stopped her and asked her where the accessible entrance was. Good news—there was one, but I needed to go back outside and go around the other side of the building again. Now normally, for the very reason that is about to unfold, I'm hyper-aware of what's around me. But this time, I was stressed about my interview and in my haste, I turned my head *and* my chair in the direction the security guard gestured. As you've probably predicted by now, there was a curb *right behind me,* so when I turned, my front wheels went down. Right off the curb, catapulting me out of my chair and onto the cement parking garage floor below me. It wasn't graceful. It wasn't a cute little tumble. It was something akin to a muppet tumbling down from their perch. So embarrassing.

Now let me pause for a second and tell you. This could have been so much worse. I have seen time and time again in my life that I truly, 100% have the best guardian angel in the universe. See what happened was, before I got to the parking garage, I'd found another door. I stopped two women who looked like they were on their way back to work from lunch and asked them to open the door. Stairs. I asked them if they knew the building or where in the actual hell the accessible entrance was, but they didn't. They were very kind and started walking with me in the direction of the garage to try to help me find the door. This will become important in just a second.

Fast-forward, I am lying on the ground, looking up at my chair teetering over me. I had growing pain in my right arm and knew something was wrong. Very wrong, in fact. The two women and the security guard had rushed to me and were asking me how they could help. It was a pickle. My electric chair weighed 300 pounds and was half on the curb, half off. I was ALL THE WAY on the ground, and I knew I was injured. We decided we needed an ambulance and when they arrived, they assessed pretty quickly that my arm was likely broken (eh-hem, it was actually broken in TWO places—right above my elbow and right below my shoulder. I am an overachiever, if you recall and when I do something, I do it spectacularly, thank you very much!).

I am a tricky person to move WITHOUT a broken arm—I have bad hips and knees and so I started talking with the paramedics and the women about what might be the best way to get me onto the stretcher. One of the women leaned over, took my hand and said, "Just so you know, I'm an occupational therapist so I have a lot of experience with moving people and with wheelchairs, so I've got you."

What? Of all the people on the street that day, I stopped an occupational therapist right before injuring myself and needing help being transferred AND getting my wheelchair to safety until my husband could go pick it up? That was a miracle if ever I've seen one.

She was true to her word. She helped the paramedics get me on the stretcher. She made sure I had my personal belongings. She called my husband AND helped the security guard get my wheelchair safely into a storage closet where it could remain until my husband could pick it up. AND, she and her friend went up and told the gentleman I was supposed to interview with what had happened so I wasn't just a no-show.

Sometimes, the things that suck allow you to see the kindness and humanity in people. This is not the only such example I have and these kinds of interactions with people have made me 100% certain and unwavering in my belief that people are basically good and kind and here to help if and when they can. There are people in the mix, of course, who are not kind, but I believe—for the most part, people in this world are kind and compassionate.

Now, that was an extreme example of the consequences when things are not made to be inclusive for me or others with physical disabilities. But the example serves to illustrate that there *are* consequences to exclusion. *This* exclusion, of course, came in the form of a building—actual architecture that excludes people who use wheelchairs—whether a permanent disability or an injured person who needs to use a wheelchair temporarily. This kind of exclusion can affect the elderly. There are accessibility issues in buildings around our cities that affect and exclude people who are visually impaired or hearing impaired.

There are all kinds of other ways people are excluded from each other, places or events that YOU may have experienced. We can be excluded from social groups—maybe we didn't get that invitation to the party or to lunch or to girls' night. We can be excluded in professional settings—passed over for promotions, excluded from a meeting or a decision we should have participated in. Sometimes women are faced with "boys club" cultures at work. We can be excluded from sports—not picked for the team, or benched. When I go on vacation with my family or friends, there are all kinds of things I am excluded from. Tons of sightseeing options are off the table for me because there is no accessible transportation to allow me to get to the destinations. There are a million other examples of ways *you* may have felt excluded from something in your life.

Air travel. Oh, my sweet baby Jesus. Today, it boggles my mind how we have not brought air travel into this century to be more inclusive for people with physical limitations to navigate. For a person who uses a wheelchair, like me, air travel is actually quite dehumanizing, and I don't use that term lightly. There is no excuse why, in today's day and age, I should not be able to drive my wheelchair onto an airplane.

I am not unreasonable, I promise you. I understand the engineering to make aircrafts accessible to the point of being able to drive a wheelchair onto the plane and have space for it, is tricky. I know that every nail and bolt and screw must serve a purpose. But tricky is not impossible. Hard, yes? Impossible, NO. Solve the problem. Help people who use wheelchairs to be able to travel as safely and comfortably, AND with as much dignity as anyone else.

Currently, I have to be handled and lifted by people I don't know and who are not trained in *my* personal limitations and do not know how to move me without injuring me (not to mention the invasion of my person, being touched and lifted by strangers.). I have to be transferred by them to an aisle chair—often times in front of other passengers—strapped in like I am going parachuting, hauled down the aisle of the plane in this chair, in front of onlookers, and then transferred again *by strangers* into my airplane seat. Then, they take my $30,000 wheelchair down below to store with the luggage—tossed in and out of the plane with no regard to the fact that if it turns up broken on the other end, they've essentially broken my legs. This is truly humiliating all the way around and needs to be fixed.

But, regardless of the *variety* of exclusion we're talking about, the subtext is the same—you're not wanted. You're not welcome. You're not a priority here. You're not good enough to matter or to be here. You're not important enough for us to create a way for you to exist in this space. You're inconvenient. You don't matter as much as someone else. You're not fun, smart, or talented enough. So many messages can be sent between the lines of exclusion. And what suffers is usually our self-esteem.

So, like I've said before in other chapters, let's not be a victim here, friends. We clearly understand that exclusion happens. Exclusion sucks. We all get left out in the cold sometimes. And there is no disputing the messages we are being sent in the act of being excluded from any situation. For our very human hearts, those messages hurt.

First. Try turning what I just said on its ear. Sometimes the message being sent IS an intentional one. Sometimes it IS malicious or egregious. But a lot of the time, it's not. Also, if it is intended, malicious or egregious, do we have to receive it that way?

We don't have to allow the exclusions in our lives to rule. In the context of exclusion in the form of accessibility, I choose to, first, hold love in my heart for the individuals who created that space, and recognize that I don't necessarily know anything about the circumstances around which the space was built. Was it pre-1973? Were they uneducated about accessibility? Were they intentionally defiant? I often don't know the answer, and I acknowledge that. Even if it was intentional and I KNOW it was, is that the important data point to my situation? Because if it *was* intentional, that person has a flaw in their wiring and that's THEIR problem in life, not mine, and I won't let it become my problem.

What I believe the important data point is, is that it's wrong, it's exclusion and it should be fixed, *and* people should do better. So, I empower myself to talk about it. I control and influence what I can. I look for opportunities to speak about inclusion and accessible design. I put my energy into fixing the problem and being part of the solution instead of being angry and frustrated. Guess which one feels better for me?

The person who built the space doesn't know if I am sitting around being angry. If I do, it becomes the metaphorical drinking of poison and hoping the other person will die. The other person is going on about their life (not caring if I am angry and have blood-pressure issues because of their insensitivity), and they *may be* building more structures where I can influence the way it's built if I use my time constructively, bring positive attention to the issue (I choose not to shame people—I speak about it from a progressive, positive place, because shame begets shame and only breeds more exclusion) and help make people aware of what they are perpetuating. Now, THAT feels a lot better than being angry and feeling sorry for myself.

How does this land with you? Whenever I am faced with a problem, regardless of the problem's variety, the second I take action is when I start to feel better. This topic is no different. Are there areas in your life where you've felt excluded and could take this approach? Try coming at these things with a positive, generous, solution-oriented mindset and see where that leads.

The famous Martin Luther King, Jr. quote is coming to mind here, "Darkness cannot drive out darkness, only light can do that. Hate cannot drive out hate, only love can do that." Now, while I realize what I am talking about here may not be as extreme as darkness and hate, or maybe it is, but, I believe the words still ring true.

Any time I am faced with some form of inequality, injustice, adversity, etc., I try to approach it from a place of positivity and light. Because I don't believe that more hate and more shame solve problems. Positivity, understanding, authenticity, and empowerment do. Even if you ARE dealing with a horrible person, maybe your grace will have an impact on them and how they conduct themselves in the future. It could happen!

Another phrase is coming to mind, my mom often quoted her child-hood friend, Corinthia, to me in difficult times. Her friend would often say, "I can out-class anyone." And it's true. This has become a mantra for me in life and I'VE quoted it to MY daughter, my employees, friends, etc. I choose to take the high road and be the bigger person and help fix problems that cross my path. There is usually no downside to being kind and generous, even if that's not the same treatment I've been given. Some may call it weakness. I call it strength that in the face of situations like these I'm able to get back up, smile, and approach the problem with kindness.

Are there circumstances of exclusion in your life where you can extrapolate anything from this and empower yourself to *be* the change? *Be* the solution, even if you didn't cause the problem? Even if the problem is something that was done to you? Where *you* were wronged? It's powerful stuff, my friends.

And finally, let's look at the personal side of exclusion. Those times when we feel (or are overtly) excluded from a social or professional situation—a party, a club, a promotion, a clique. I don't typically handle these situations much differently.

One time, I was at an All-Hands offsite day-long meeting where the entire company I worked with gathered once a year. It was the end of the day and everyone was celebrating. There was a band, and a dance floor, and an open bar.

I sat talking with another woman who I worked with, I was actually her assigned mentor at the time and she was relatively new to the company. Soon, about three other women ran over, physically pulled her to her feet and off to dance with them. I was left sitting at the table feeling foolish and alone. It would have been nice to have been pulled along with her. Maybe they didn't know if I could dance. Maybe they were trying to include her since she was new. I would have liked to have been included too.

It hurts. I get it. I always try to start with, "I don't know what they were thinking when they made the decision they made." And it's true. I didn't. I could have pursued it and asked, but I didn't want to make someone else feel bad. Maybe they deserved to feel bad; I chose not to be the spoilsport in the moment.

What I typically choose is this—to be myself. To CONTINUE to be myself. If these are people who I want to include me going forward, I try to be a person they *want* to include and try to make it known that I *can be* included. If not, I don't sweat it.

Life is full of people who are just insensitive. When they behave insensitively, that is more data. Are they someone, based on that, who I want to try again with? Or does it tell me they might not be "my people?" I've had both scenarios in life. AND, there are times when I've given people the benefit of the doubt and second chances to who didn't deserve them, and then I moved on. Again—*their* insensitivity doesn't have to be my problem. I am who I am and I am capable of getting myself included where I want to be.

Bottom line—we are in control of how we respond in these situations in life where we are excluded in one way or another. I haven't always handled every situation perfectly, but if there's one thing in life I've learned—I am responsible for who I am and how I behave and react. Even in, maybe *especially,* in times where others have treated me badly.

Chapter 16:
Feeling Lost

One time, years ago, I got lost in Austin. I was coming home from a date in a part of town I was super unfamiliar with. It was pre-GPS and navigation on our phones (it was, like, the "olden-days!"), and the guy had hand written directions to get me home on a sheet of paper. I got in my car and started to drive. I'd memorized the first two or three steps to get me home, but it was kind of a convoluted set of directions, and then I realized—it was too dark to read the rest of the directions in my car. I couldn't turn on the interior light because I use both my hands to drive—one hand to steer and the other hand to work the gas and brake.

I pulled over, and as I did, the paper with the directions slithered off the front seat, like it was slow motion. From my wheelchair in the front seat, I didn't have the reach to bend down and pick them up. I didn't have the guy's number programmed into my phone, and it was about midnight—too late to be calling people like a fool to ask directions.

I sat there for a few minutes and considered my options. There weren't many. So, I took stock of the few turns I'd taken to get to where I was and tried to place myself near some landmark. Nothing. I truly, genuinely, had no idea where I was.

So, I started to drive. At this point my thought process was, "I'll drive until I see something familiar, then I'll know where to go." Eventually, with a little luck on my side, it worked, and I did make it home.

Another time, I was in the Dallas area for my nephew's baptism. I am not from there and hadn't spent a lot of time there driving around.

Fortunately, this was just *after* cell phones started having GPS systems in them, and I was excited to hop in the car that morning at the hotel and use my shiny new GPS app to get to the church. Unfortunately, it was an overcast day and there was construction—EVERYWHERE—screwing with the GPS's connection AND its computer of maps. First-generation—anything—is always a little dicey, and just as I got too far away from the hotel to find my way back there, the GPS went kablooey. No. More. Directions.

I panicked. Seriously. I was in a huge city I didn't know and my little trick of driving until something looked familiar could have landed me in Oklahoma. My daughter, who was 10 at the time I think, was in the car with me, so I settled on deep-breathing, and crying as quietly as possible to keep from completely freaking out in the front seat, so as not to freak her out in the back seat. Eventually, we found a place to pull over to ask for some directions and then, my GPS kicked back in and we got to the church safely, only missing part of his baptism. UGH.

Yes. These are, in fact, metaphors for being lost in life. But the tactics can still apply. I've been in places in my life several times where I've felt lost. Where I didn't really know who I was anymore, didn't know what I wanted, and certainly didn't know why I was here and what I was meant to do.

After I got married, I felt very lost after a time. I was trying to redefine myself from a single woman to a married one. Then, I became a mother. When you add people and these permanent relationships to your life, it causes you to change or evolve into a new person who now exists with these other people. I was not my first priority anymore. When these life-changes happen, we suddenly have a person or people besides ourselves to answer to and to make decisions with. What you do affects them. You don't have the carefree life of going off on a girl's weekend, or hitting happy hour every Friday after work anymore, or spending money however you see fit. Your dreams and wants can become threats to *their* happiness and security, so sometimes, I think we feel like we have to give them up like a "responsible adult," and live life by the rules. Whatever that means.

I think our upbringing, or the friends we have and the circles we are in, and the role models we have, sometimes dictate what the rules are. I had a very traditional upbringing. My mom was a teacher, and then when my sister and I were born, she stayed home with us. My dad worked outside the home and it was a great upbringing. I felt safe and supported and never went without anything.

Because of my disability and the life I knew I had always wanted— a home, a car, kids, pets, the occasional vacation, and then to be able to pay for personal care assistants (upwards of $2,500-3,000 a month), deductibles on $30,000 wheelchairs, doctor's appointments, etc., I had to work—a really good job. Being disabled, it turns out, is very expensive without factoring in anything else like lifestyle, so I had to keep working after we adopted our daughter, and so in my mind, I was already deviating from the rules a little. I loved that my mom was always there with us when we were kids, and I felt guilty for having to work.

It was a 9-5 corporate life, and a family whose happiness was my first priority. I became last on a lot of lists in my own mind. I gained a ton of weight, and didn't feel good about myself physically—I'd gotten healthy and lost and kept off so much weight in my twenties and so I felt like I'd failed at the one thing I could do for myself such as keeping myself healthy and looking a way I was proud of.

I am going to pause here for a second and acknowledge that I suspect what I am describing is what a lot of people reading this have experienced. I think this is a fairly common tale for a lot of women. And I will say it for ALL of us—we love our families—our spouses, our kids— fiercely and would never trade them for anything. I love being a wife and a mother, but there is something about it for a lot of women that causes us, in that act of prioritizing others, to de-prioritizing ourselves. And, by extension, to lose ourselves.

Though I am not a man, I am sure the idea of losing ourselves is also a thing for them. They also become part of something bigger than just themselves when they have a family and must reprioritize.

There are ways we can lose ourselves in our jobs—family or no. Sometimes our careers go in directions we never expected and didn't decide on with intention. We just go along for the ride and follow our careers where they take us. I hear people say they wake up one morning and 30 years have gone by and they have nothing to show for it. Or, that life got away from them and they're not sure how they landed where they are.

Abusive relationships—worthy of mention, but it's a lay person's opinion. Suffice it to say, though, that these are relationships that I know are quite typical of someone losing themselves somewhere and becoming a shell of who they used to be.

And what about people who go through periods in their life when they are evaluating gender identity and what that means for their lives and their relationships. Younger people who go to college for the first time, or move from one school to another, or are trying to figure out what to study and what to do with the rest of their lives. People who get divorced and begin life again. People who are widowed. So many scenarios where we de-prioritize ourselves, or become confused for one reason or another, or just lose our connection with our center and who we are and what we want.

I think the important thing to say here is that, if this is where you are in life right now, you are not alone. Not even close. That is why it is a chapter in this book unto itself. I chose the 17 things in life that I believe are so prevalent in the number of people they suck for and the universality of the topics, and this is one of them. A LOT of people feel how you feel. I have felt how you feel. But there is good news—you don't have to feel this way forever. It's possible to shake free of it and find yourself again. You're still in there. And you matter, too.

Let's go back to my example of being lost, geographically. In the first scenario I described, I kept going until something looked familiar and it all worked itself out and made my way home and I got back on course. I spent a lot of time on this kind of autopilot in my life. I wasn't aware that I was lost, until something woke me up and I realized that I was living life on autopilot and, beneath the surface, I was hoping that something would come along again sometime to remind me of the person who used to have dreams and goals—something to make me interesting again. I can remember a time when I thought I'd lived all my dreams and goals and that was all I got. Sound familiar?

Guess what? We decide when we're done dreaming and have hit every goal that interests us. There is no expiration date on wanting things. On wanting to do and experience and *be* things.

There were times when something did come along. A job opportunity, usually. Even when I was feeling lost as a person, I was ambitious in my career, and so when opportunities for promotions or to try something new came along, I'd often go for it. Sometimes it worked out, sometimes it didn't. When it did, it gave me something new to focus on for a while, but I still felt like there was something missing, deep in the essence of who I was a lot of the time. But I kept going, following the rules I thought I was supposed to follow.

And looking back now, I can see what a mistake this was. FOR ME, not for everyone, but for me, I knew there was something I had turned off inside of me. A sparkle was gone, and I was going through a lot of motions because I thought it was what I was *supposed* to do.

I also can see that I was robbing my family of some of who I was. I tamed it because I thought I had to, but that was the exact opposite of the model and the example my daughter needed. It was the opposite of what would have been good for my relationship with my husband.

So now, let's bring in my second example of when I got lost in Dallas. I cried. I was intentional about not scaring my daughter, but I felt the frustration and the fear. I stopped the car, we got directions and the GPS came back on line and we made it to our destination.

This is kind of what happened when I lost my last corporate job. That was the metaphorical GPS going offline. I job hunted on autopilot for a while because that was what I thought I was supposed to do, and then, I got frustrated. I realized how lost I was. I cried and I felt the feels and I got intentional about solving the problem. I realized that the only other thing I could do was follow my passions while I job hunted. And guess what? My passions came from that place inside of me I'd forgotten about—the place that lit me up. And when I found that place again, everything got easier. AND it didn't make me a worse wife or mother because I was focusing on what lit me up, it made me a happier one. My daughter is 20, and I am so excited to finally be modeling the kind of woman I hope she will be. One who knows herself. Who does things her way. Who does what she LOVES. Who manages to love her people, but also keep true to herself.

Finally.

One more analogy for you. If you are craving pizza, you can go through the day on autopilot, hoping one will show up at your door. OR, you can go to the website, look through the toppings and see which ones get you excited, and you can place the order. Which of those options will get the pizza to your door?

Intention is the key. Like I said, you're still in there. What excites and lights you up may be the same as it was 20 years ago, maybe it's not. Like Marie Forleo says, though, "Everything is figuroutable." Spend some time with it. Journal. Meditate. Pay attention to what is crossing your path and be open. Instead of walking around believing this is it, wake up every morning and remind yourself that the world is full of people and places and possibilities. Go on a date with your kids or your partner and play the "what if" game. Dream. Dreaming is not committing, so have fun with it. It might be the first step toward figuring out what you want again. If you have a dream you *cannot* let go of, it may be more than a dream. It may be a calling. That is 100% what writing this book and being a speaker was for me. It was there, in the back of my mind for 15 years. I pushed it down again and again and again saying, "I can't. Moms don't leave good careers to be a motivational speaker. It's too late. I don't know how."

Turns out, I can. Mom's DO leave careers and build new ones. It wasn't too late, and, I figured it out. If there is any doubt in your mind that you can do what you've always wanted to do, look at the proof in your hands. You're reading it. People say this all the time, "If I can do it, you can do it." But guys—for real, if I can do it, you can do it. Your path won't look like mine, but you can figure it out. I am a living, breathing contradiction. In some ways, because of my physical limitations, I need and depend on people the same ways a baby does. And yet, I want to command rooms, and motivational-speak people and kick the crap out of limitations and get to the possibilities. And I did. You can too.

This ended up being SUCH a calling for me that my GPS had to go offline in my life—I had to "be invited to leave" my job and be refused 53 other jobs to get me to pay freaking attention and do what I was meant to.

It doesn't matter how you get back to self. Decide you will and create a path.

Chapter 17:
Disappointment

Disappointment is the outcome of something not meeting your hopes or expectations. I remember the day that I found out the first treatment EVER for my neuromuscular disease had been approved.

It was December 23, 2016. We'd just had friends over for a holiday dinner, and after I got into bed, I opened my laptop and decided to catch up on email. The headline of the email caught my attention immediately. "FDA Approves First Drug for Spinal Muscular Atrophy." My vision blurred and I felt like I was having an out-of-body experience. I knew researchers were making some good progress and that a promising treatment was likely to come soon, but there it was. In print. Two days before Christmas. I started to cry just as my husband walked in. I couldn't even tell him what was wrong. I pointed at the screen and told him to read. It was my miracle. Sometimes, though, things don't go according to plan…

I was 43 years old at the time, and over the years, I'd watched my body get weaker, experienced the loss of function—things like reaching my arm up to put mascara on, or lift a glass up to drink from. The older I got, the more quickly I was losing function and, I won't lie, I was terrified.

As I read, I learned the new treatment was an injection that had to go into the spinal fluid. There were four "loading doses" that had to be injected within the first 60 days and then one injection would be required indefinitely every 3 months. Oh, and also—each dose was about $125,000.

Okay, so it wasn't going to be the super-fun pill I could swallow with my morning coffee, which is what I'd always hoped for. And the price tag…wow…but none of that mattered. I would have robbed a bank and hung upside down by my toenails while the medicine was injected into my eyeballs if I'd had to.

I also read that they'd being taking phone calls to answer questions and provide information that Monday. Guess what I did Monday morning at 8:30 am?? I did not pass "Go," did not collect $200. I called the dang number.

I was told, however, that the rollout of the medication could take a little time and would have to be coordinated with my neurologist. Okay, I'd waited this long. Next phone call was to my neurologist who was on vacation for two weeks. COME ON—didn't he know he couldn't be on vacation on the day my miracle was granted? I could wait a little longer.

Fast-forward "some" time—I finally found myself sitting in my neurologist's office with my husband. The news wasn't what I'd hoped for. More hoops to jump through. There were forms he was going to have to fill out with the pharmaceutical company AND I needed a blood test his office could not give me to reconfirm my neuromuscular diagnosis. Never mind the fact that I'd been diagnosed via a muscle biopsy when I was an infant.

They needed *this* test.

I get it.

We needed to be thorough, and like I'd said, I had waited 43 years already.

Fast-forward a few more months, paperwork done, and diagnosis confirmed. But then, there were two additional hurdles. The price tag and my insurance. Fortunately, there was a financial assistance program the pharmaceutical company offered if your insurance wouldn't cover it, but my insurance had to deny me three times, and we had to appeal the denial. Three times.

Finally, I was approved for the financial assistance program (shocker—insurance denied it! Three times.), but there was one other small thing, that wasn't so small.

The FDA approved the medication for people with my condition, of all ages. Exactly what I wanted. And yet—the drug trials hadn't included anyone over the age of 17. They'd gotten great results for kids, but for a (by this time) 44-year-old woman, whose condition had progressed an additional 30 years and whose muscles had had 30 more years to atrophy, no one knew what to expect. No doctor could tell me if the medication would be of any benefit to me. I told my doctor I wanted to try. There were no concerning side effects to be worried about, so I didn't see the downside.

He got to work trying to schedule the injection. It couldn't be done in his office, though. Because my spine had been fused when I was 14 to correct scoliosis, and my back was full of rods and wires and screws, the procedure needed to be done with some very sophisticated imaging equipment. Months went by. Between the price tag, the fact that there was no protocol for the procedure for an adult, no facilities in Austin were doing it. More months went by.

Finally, my doctor and I decided to try looking outside Austin, and found a doctor near Houston who said he would do it. He was a pain management doctor and did lots of tricky epidurals and things and had a fluoroscopy machine that should give him the visibility he needed to guide the needle into my spine. But first, I had to drive to Houston just for an intake appointment to be able to book the procedure. Ugh.

Check, check, check, and Holy-toledo-check-already. I'd jumped through all the hoops and done all the things. The day had come—about 15 months after the FDA approved my miracle.

I got to Houston, checked in, got transferred onto a stretcher, rode into the fluoroscopy room, and was transferred again onto a table. The doctor came in. He briefly explained what he was going to do. There was a gigantic machine that moved all the way around me and projected images onto screens. The doctor went to work.

And then, he stopped. Turns out, my body's response to the spine being fused and all the hardware put into it was a ton of boney growth collecting over a lot of that hardware, and there was no way for the doctor to get the needle into my spinal fluid. He tried—holy cow, did he try. He went in and out and pushed and prodded, hoping for a minuscule opening he could get through.

Nothing. There was 100%, absolutely no way he was getting in. I wanted to beg him to keep trying, but I refrained. We left—there was a Mexican restaurant next door and we decided to have lunch before heading back to Austin. I sat at the table having another out-of-body experience. The menu blurred before me because of the tears in my eyes. I could not understand why this was happening and HOW there could be a treatment that existed, but that we could not get into my body. There are no words for the disappointment I felt on that day. I had arrived in Houston with hope in my heart, believing I would be leaving Houston with this medicine coursing through me for the first time.

Instead, I left Houston feeling like I'd been diagnosed with this condition all over again. I was so sad, so discouraged and so…SO disappointed.

I regrouped with my neurologist, and he assured me it could be done—we just needed even more sophisticated imaging equipment, and probably a Neuro-interventional radiologist—who knew THAT was a thing?? Talk about specific!

More months went by, and then—we were set to try again. A hospital in Houston, a BIG facility with crazy-sophisticated equipment and the best of the best doctors doing these injections for adults. SO, I had to transfer neurologists to one in Houston who had permissions at that hospital and could write the order. Off my fanny went to Houston AGAIN for my intake appointment with her. And when we were done—she said she could schedule it for the following week. Wait. I wouldn't have to wait two more months for an appointment? She laughed at my surprise and actually said, "You've been through so much. We want to make it as easy as possible for you." She gave me her email address. A NEUROLOGIST gave me her personal email address. Was she for real?? Things were looking up.

The day came—again. We didn't know what to expect of the day, so we'd booked a hotel near the hospital and come in the night before. The next morning, we got to the hospital, got checked in and went to the *first* waiting area—where we waited. A long time.

Then, we were shown to the triage area. There were consent forms. There were doctors to talk to. Turns out, there was confusion over the approach—were they going in through my neck or my lower spine— apparently that changed a lot of the details, so it had to be sorted out. Meanwhile, they started an IV on me so they could give me pain medi- cation because I was going to have to lie in a fairly painful position for the spinal injection. I am here to tell you. I have the worst veins on the planet. You may *think* yours are the worst. They're not. I will win at this game all day long. They tried an ultrasound machine at one point to help guide the needle—to no avail. They had to locate and call in the ONE woman in the hospital they referred to as "the vein whisperer." She was magnificent and finally, IV in, I was ready.

And then, they checked my blood pressure, which was approximately 235/190. Are you kidding me?? They spent a couple hours getting my blood pressure down and stable. There was talk of me maybe needing to stay overnight. Then, at 4 pm they came in and said we could go in. OMG. I SO thought the day was going to end and that they were going to postpone it. But they didn't. We went in, got me on the table and into the very painful position. They ended up having to do the injection via CT scan. The doctor took a bunch of images with the CT machine to figure out where he thought he could get in, working around the hard- ware and the extra boney growth around it. Then, he started the needle going in. Then, they fed me back into the CT machine, checked the angle and trajectory of the needle, the doctor made some corrections and went in further. BACK into the CT machine to check, back out, more adjust- ments, back in. About 10 times we did this.

I was in some pain and was nauseous from the blood pressure medica- tion they'd given me. One of the doctors (there were three in the room for this, plus a nurse and a tech or three) came around the side of the table I was facing and held my hand. He told me they were almost there, and told me a really, really bad joke I'll spare you from. And then, he said, very casually, "Okay, two more minutes, the medicine is going in." I blinked and looked up at him and said, "It's going in???" He realized, I think, the gravity of the moment, squeezed my hand and said, "Yes. It is." And I started to cry. 45 years old now, and almost two years after the treatment was approved, it was going IN to my body.

It's been about three years now that I've been getting these injections. They've gotten easier, AND I'm now able to get them from another fantastic team in Austin. We've figured out what works best for me—each person is a little different, of course—and now, when I go in, I'm in and out in about two hours. We've figured out how to best manage the discomfort, and the doctor is very familiar with my "tricky" anatomy and knows very well how to navigate it. He's also one of the nicest guys I've ever met.

I realize as I am writing this, there may be other people out there considering this treatment and I want to say, with my whole entire heart, while my path to get here was incredibly challenging, please don't let my story and experience scare you off from trying this treatment. Obviously, it's you and your doctor's call what you do. But don't use my story as a data point not to get it. It's been five years now since this medicine was approved, and we've worked out the kinks! You won't have to go through all the challenges I did that come with new medicines, creating proto-cols from scratch and working through the insurance red tape, and the doctors and the facilities' administrative processes to create and approve everything. While it wouldn't be my pick of procedures to have done, like I said, I would agree to do far worse to get access to it. It's SO worth it—I can do hard things, and so can you! Be a warrior!!

Three years in, and I can tell you the progression of my condition has stopped, AND I've gained some subtle strength back. It's not a cure, but to know it's stopped the illness from getting worse is SO worth it. So again, don't use my story here as fuel to feed your fear. Use it as fuel to feed your courage to do something brave for yourself, even if it's hard.

Even though this endeavor was ultimately a success—and a dream come true, at that—it was a long, emotional road of disappointment after CRUSHING disappointment.

What I remember most is the frustration. I didn't understand why people couldn't just see the logic behind how to make this procedure happen. I am not a health care administrator, of course (which was pointed out to me along the way), but I know business. I grew up in hospitals. I'd had a lifetime career of having procedures done and of being in doctors' offices. I knew how to advocate for myself. My father ran hospitals, and I spent a lot of time in his office. I could see the vision of what needed to happen but was being told I didn't understand. Maybe I didn't FULLY understand. It didn't make it any less frustrating to not be taken seriously or to have this miracle withheld for two years.

Disappointment. I've been, as I am sure you have, disappointed so many times in my life. I've been disappointed by friends. I've been disappointed by jobs I didn't get. I've been disappointed by boys and men. I've been disappointed by the continued inaccessibility of the world. I've disappointed myself when I've made a bad decision or a mistake.

But I think disappointment is a lot like so many other things in life that suck. There is opportunity and purpose there if we want to see it.

When I look back on this experience. I got some skills from it. I was already pretty good at advocating for myself after (like I said) a lifetime of working with doctors and learning what I needed, what worked for me and what didn't. But THIS took my self-advocacy to a new level. I thought I was determined. This took my determination to a new level. I thought I was resourceful. Yup—new level.

I think of the unique circumstances surrounding these events, my crazy anatomy and all the complications that arose. And I choose to believe the doctors who worked with me—who were all very good—might be even better now, having worked on me. The techs, the nurses—all of them had a part in working with me and working around some of the unique circumstances I brought to their day. The administrators who had to, eventually, get behind this procedure and figure out how to make it happen—maybe they learned some things from this challenging experience, and maybe next time, they will be better prepared and equipped to work through the process more quickly.

Of course, we can be angry and let disappointment after disappointment in life beat us down. Wrapped up in disappointment is a lot of deeper emotion. Disappointments can color how we feel about people, whether we trust people, whether we believe in ourselves and try again. Like so many other things in life—what I ask myself is, "Is that how you want to live? Being mistrustful and jaded?" That is not how I want to live.

I have seen some hideous examples of people who have let other people down. And I have seen people's mindsets and how they approach the world be completely changed as a result. Know who that hurts? Only themselves. The other person has moved on and doesn't care if you are jaded or mistrustful.

The other things I think disappointments can teach us is critical thinking. There is a big difference, my friends, between caution and critical thinking and complete mistrust and pessimism about the world at large.

Even if you see a trend. The trend doesn't have to be representative of ALL people. I try, despite the let downs and the disappointments I've experienced in my lifetime, to treat every person and every situation in my life as a unique one. I evaluate things in the new situation based on the information I have from past experiences and disappointments. I know I can make better, more informed decisions based on what I know because of what I've been through.

I look for the good and I hope for the best. I use critical thinking to understand and act and respond, and I try for good outcomes. Does it mean that sometimes I get disappointed again? Of course. If I am—I process that disappointment. Learn what I can from it (including how I can do better next time), and I try to move on.

Sometimes that's easier than other times, but I DO NOT WANT to turn into the angry pessimist. Who wants to spend time with them?? And if that person is you, there is no escape!

Disappointments can ruin your day six ways from Tuesday. But you are stronger than the disappointment. Feel those feels. I needed to cry after that first attempt to get the medicine into my spine that failed. Honor your disappointment and frustration, let it be, but then be selfish and take what you can from it. Like so many other things I've talked about in this book, let it teach you and make you a better person. At the end of the day, what is going to matter in all of this is the person you are and how you show up.

Take your punches. Get back up. Next time, you'll have a better strategy for avoiding the punch in the first place—or in receiving the punch so it hurts less.

Epilogue:
Limitations

Most people in this world don't have enough of what they would like to have. For me, I have limited physical abilities. The ability to walk, to stand, to run, to pick things up, to ride roller coasters. I have limited cash flow. Limited ability to take all the trips I would like to take, limits on the number and amount of charitable donations I'd like to make, limits on the number of shoes and jewelry I'd like to buy. I have limits to my professional connections (I'll take that introduction to Oprah ANY time, y'all…).

We ALL have limitations bestowed upon us, but there is a give-and-take. You may be able to run a marathon, but not be able to pay your electric bill. That guy over there may have millions to give to charity, but no friends to wish him a happy birthday.

I mentioned earlier in this book that I had the opportunity to speak with Shawn Achor and pick his brain about some of the topics I'm writing about, and I just listened back to the interview again and just 30 minutes with him gave me so much that I'd like to impart to you in this final chapter of the book. So much of what he and I discussed came down to mindset and tools we can use to break free of deficit mindsets we sometimes get stuck in when bad things happen.

Quick story—when I was three or four years old, my mom had a neighbor-friend over who I guess asked me what I wanted to be when I grew up. I looked at her, and without missing a beat, I said, "tap dancer."

Where in the ever-loving heck this came from, none of us knew. She could have asked me for some other ideas, or prompted me to come up with anything else I might want to do. She could have helped me understand that I had limitations that would prevent that dream—no matter how fleeting—from coming true. But instead, the next time she came over, she brought me a pair of tap shoes. We had a wooden sandbox in the backyard and my mom took me out there, wiped away the sand from the bottom of one corner of the sandbox, plopped me down on the side of the sandbox and let me tap my feet to my heart's content.

One of the things Shawn and I talked about is our belief and action systems. Usually, when something bad happens, we need to have some kind of belief that something can be okay or can be different or better before we can take action to actually make it better or different. In this story, our neighbor and my mom gave me that belief. I already couldn't stand or walk. To take away the belief that I could be a tap dancer might have kept me stuck in a three-year-old mindset of pessimism about what I could and could not do. I was going to figure out one day that being a tap dancer was not a viable option for me, but the belief in that moment that I could, tapping away in the sandbox gave me the belief that I *was* a tap dancer and in that, I found joy. AND, I would argue that because more limitations were not placed upon me, my ability to "action" through life and kick the heck out of my other goals despite my physical limitations was allowed to exist.

I think that one of the coolest things my parents did for me was NOT to place *more* limitations on me because of my disability. Even though I had limitations on my body, they didn't let that bleed over into limitations on my life. In fact, they had a lot of expectations of me.

I have an able-bodied sister and their expectations for both of us were the same. We were expected to do well in school, to try, to work hard, to behave (dangit!), to have interests and to pursue them. I had chores, like my sister did. I had to keep my room cleaned up and set the dinner table because even if I couldn't clean a bathroom, I could wheel in a circle around a table and put silverware and napkins at each spot.

I recognize that I was fortunate to grow up in the family that I did, and I am so grateful. Because I credit their expectations with helping me to see beyond what I might have thought my limitations were and stopped there. Instead, I became a person who has managed to accomplish *almost* every goal I ever set for myself (I never won a Grammy, but I DID earn a master's degree).

Listen up—most of us in this world *know* our true limitations or will figure them out. And a lot of us will far exceed what others thought our limits would keep us from pulling off. DO NOT PRESUME TO KNOW ANYONE ELSE'S LIMITS. You don't want to be that guy, I promise. Let people exceed your expectations and conquer their dreams. If my parents had sat me down and had a talk about how I couldn't be a tap dancer—but maybe I could be good at math—well, I would have completely failed at life because then I would have been both discouraged AND learned that I, too, sucked at math. You have no right—despite what you think you might know—to be the keeper of dreams and limitations and to decide who gets which. So, don't. Ever. Soapbox complete.

So, what do we do with these limitations we have in our lives, our bodies, our bank accounts, our Rolodexes (if you're younger than 35, Google Rolodex. Hint, it's not a watch)? I think the first thing we can do is test the limit. I did—I tried the tap shoes, but you could only tap so much sitting stationary at the corner of a sandbox. Eventually, I figured out that this *was* a permanent limitation and I needed a new plan. Check it out. Some things are fixable. You can make more money. You can get more education. You can grow your network. You can improve aspects of your heath. Think outside that box and if there's a way to eliminate or *go around* the limitation, do it! Even if it takes a year of networking, a second job, finishing that degree, some limits can be lifted, if you're willing to *believe* something different is possible AND to put the *action* behind it to make it so.

There are also permanent, "truly nothing anyone can do about them" limitations—my disability. Business decisions made outside your span of control. A death in your family. The world around you. But, even in the face of my permanent physical limitations, I've claimed the word "limitless" as my life's philosophy. Because I don't believe in many limitations—I believe in potential.

It can be a good place to start if you acknowledge whether your own limitation is something you can change or not. This can help you take that next step. If you can't change it, you can move on and focus your life and your efforts on things where you *have* assets and capabilities. If you CAN change a limitation you currently have with some effort and action, figure out if it's important to you and if it is, understand why (this will keep you motivated to make the effort to keep going until the change is made). Then make a plan and execute.

Moving on from the emotion we feel around a permanent limitation or working our way through a plan to change a limitation can take some time. What do we do in the meantime? There is plenty of opportunity along the way to get stuck, demotivated and frustrated.

There are a few tools Shawn and I discussed that can be helpful. The first one I want to talk about is gratitude. Gratitude has been an important theme in my life, and it's honestly going to be the most useful if you implement it preemptively in your life. When something goes wrong, if you practice gratitude regularly, it can pre-wire you for successful outcomes. It prepares us and sets us up with mindsets for constructive action or approaches to those challenges. In fact, according to Shawn's research, in 30 days people who committed to writing down three to five things every night that happened in the last 24 hours that they could be grateful for (three to five *unique things,* mind you), went from testing as high-level pessimists to low-level optimists. IN JUST 30 DAYS! Imagine how much different your thought patterns could be if you practiced gratitude daily for a year—or five years? I am a huge gratitude enthusiast and I highly encourage it if you're not already doing this daily. Because, if you know you're going to have to write down three things every night you were grateful for, you spend your days looking for things to be grateful for. Makes sense, eh?

Practicing gratitude also breaks us out of the pattern of scanning for and cataloging all the limitations or the things that are wrong in our lives. The bad things you may be finding on your quest may be true, but it doesn't mean that because the bad things are true, that there can't also be a million good things in our lives that are equally real and true. It takes some of the sting out of the bad things we all experience because it helps us see the good.

While we are talking about limitations, it's interesting. I've read books about people who have overcome and conquered incredibly, insanely hard things. I think to myself—I could never do that. But the thing is—we all could. These are human beings in these books. They are human beings who overcame incredible difficult, challenging things. The reason they were able to do that, though, is because they were able to look outside the challenge or the limitation and find meaning and possibilities—those are the things that can propel us forward. Shawn taught me that.

Another tool you might consider is an "in case of emergency kit." Shawn told me about a group of critical care nurses he worked with in the Boston area. As you can imagine, their jobs are very hard, very stressful and things happen all the time that are out of control—they lose patients and take care of people who, despite their best efforts, may never get better. They created kits in manila folders for themselves full of pictures kids in their care had colored for them, letters they'd received, photos patients had taken of themselves with the nurses. When they had a hard day or a hard moment, they'd pull out their "in case of emergency kit" and it helped them feel better and find hope and meaning in that moment. What could you fill your manila envelope with?

And lastly, sometimes if we have a deficit in one area of our life, we can create an abundance in another. If our professional life is in turmoil, are there social connections you can build? Go to networking events, or start a book club, or host a dinner party/barbeque/potluck. If you are having financial difficulties, can you put the pedal to the metal in your professional life? Speak with your manager and set goals to get a promotion or a raise. Take a training class and build some additional skills. Maybe what you need is some spiritual reinforcement if one part of your life is lacking. Join a church or a bible study. Create a meditation practice.

Limitations? This may be a bad analogy, but you know how they say for people who lose one sense, a heightened sense is created in another area? If you lose your sight, for example, maybe your hearing is then amplified. Same concept. Have a limitation in your life? Let that deficit drive an abundance of skill in other areas. This may not happen as naturally as amplified hearing when you lose your sight, but my goal is to bring the opportunity to your attention. With some purpose and intention, you can create abundance of skills and experience and knowledge by refocusing on other areas where you are passionate.

Life tends to be an ebb and flow in the different areas of our lives. The limitations that are placed on us could be a means of driving us in another direction or to give us the opportunity to put additional time or energy into another part of our life we've been neglecting or that could just bring us more joy than what we have now. But remember what Shawn's research has shown. We often times need a belief that there are other areas of our life that can and will provide sources of meaning and joy and fulfillment. It's okay not to be okay if life has just slapped you silly. But don't set up camp in the "I'm not okay" place. Take some baby steps and practice some gratitude or create a joy kit or list. Once you take one step and see you feel a little better, momentum builds and the action accelerates.

Our limitations may be permanent, or they may come and go, but they are a part of life. The limitation isn't the important part. The important part is what you can see, dream and work for out on the horizon despite the limitations.

For me, I saw a wheelchair I had to get into every day when I got out of bed. But I also saw a singer, and a college graduate, a goal-setter, a speaker, a writer, a *NY Times* best-selling book (have you bought a copy of this book for every single person you've ever met yet??). I saw a wife, a mother, a driver of a car, I saw a career woman, and an entrepreneur.

Those things have not been easy to accomplish. At all. But I knew what I wanted and that was so much bigger than what I didn't have to work with. I had other things to work with. I became a problem-solver. That's the thing. I learned to focus on the solution rather than the problem. I learned to create a plan. I learned to take another step, even when I didn't want to, even when it was taking too long, even when I was missing "Sex, and the City." I learned that hard work outwitted a lot of limitations I thought I had. I learned that my life didn't need to unfold how anyone else wanted it to. I learned I could do my own things my own way, and I surprised a lot of people. I love that I've surprised people and surpassed other people's expectations of me.

When you have a disability, there are so many things people out in the world don't think you can do—drive a car, be smart, date, be a parent, have physical relations, be social, be career-driven, travel, run errands. I could go on. Do you know, I've had people pat me on the head? I mean…dude.

Any time you have any limitation—there is a lot that people (including yourself!) might think you can't do. Surprise them—it's so fun! Figure out a way and don't quit.

I also HAVE TO talk about Excuses. Oy. Don't get me started! Truth bomb—excuses are nothing more than lies we tell ourselves, so we don't have to do the thing we don't want to do. You can lie to other people, but you can't lie to yourself. *You know* if you're lying. I've seen people use their limits and their challenges as excuses to not do things they didn't want to do. I've seen people use their limits or their challenges as excuses to not do things they DID want to do. What? Yep.

I've seen people so afraid of failing at a goal, or of accomplishing a goal, that they've used their challenges and limitations to not try. Guys. Adversity is not an excuse. If anything, adversity is the very *reason* we all need to get busy.

The challenges and limitations and adversity we experience in life is the best university you will ever attend. Our challenges and our limitations teach us things and give us skills we never would have had if we hadn't walked through that hard thing. At the end of that struggle, we are so much more uniquely qualified to step up and do what we want to do in life.

There is so much purpose that can come from our pain. Don't worry, I'm not going to try to convince you that everything happens for a reason. I don't even believe that. I *do* believe SOME things happen for a reason. I've already said in this book that I believe my disability was chosen for me. The only reason something would be chosen for you is because there is a purpose, and I've chosen to pursue finding that purpose. You may disagree, but I choose to believe it.

Even if we say that not everything happens for a reason, I do believe that in every challenge we face, if we *look* for purpose in it, we can find it. Sometimes a purpose is obvious, but I also believe sometimes it is a choice for us to seek and to find purpose. There is so much that happens to us in life that is hard, sad, heartbreaking, devastating. Sometimes, the hard things that happen are so exhausting, the idea of looking for purpose in them is too much to handle. Give it time.

I have spent my life, *knowing* there was a bigger purpose to all I've been through. And sometimes you do *know* it, in your bones. I believe that this book and what I have to offer people has been born of my hardest days. I believe I get to speak to audiences, and coach and have meaningful conversations on podcasts, all because I've felt the call of purpose, listened and acted on it even on my hardest days.

You may not know the purpose of what you've been through or are going through yet, but give it time. Look for it. Listen. Just because you haven't discovered it yet, doesn't mean it doesn't exist. Consider this, too—you may know the purpose and be resisting it because you don't like it.

Here's the rub—sometime the purpose isn't ours. Sometimes, the reason may be for someone you may never meet. There are cards I've been dealt along the way that I know for a fact were intended for someone else to learn a lesson. It's not always fun—to have to endure something hard so someone else can learn a lesson or find purpose. But let me tell you—when you get to see it in action, it's powerful.

Years ago, I was in Los Angeles at CBS studios to sing on the national Jerry Lewis Muscular Dystrophy Association's (MDA) telethon. I sang an original song, written by a Texas songwriter, and got to sing with their 40-piece orchestra. It was one of the biggest moments of my life, watched by approximately nine million people.

But what was even more amazing was a conversation I had with a woman in the studio the day after I'd sung. She had a ten-year-old little boy with the same neuromuscular condition as me and they were there to tell their story of how the MDA had helped them.

She told me that they had been in their hotel room the night before when I'd come on to sing. She said her little boy had been watching and that after a minute or two, he looked at her, confused, and said, "Mommy, that lady's singing on TV." She said she nodded and said, "Yes." But then he shook his head, scrunched up his face and said, "But she's in a wheel-chair." And she told me that she'd simply smiled and replied, "Yes, she is."

She said that she watched him for a few more minutes, while he watched me, and that his expression changed—he smiled, ear-to-ear. And she told me that in that moment, she knew he was realizing potential for his life he'd never seen before.

That moment made a lifetime spent in a wheelchair more than okay with me. It gave my disability a purpose, and it gave me my mission for the rest of my life—to use my struggles and what I've learned from them to help change other's experiences, lives and minds, and to help bring light and positivity to dark places. It is the moment I knew my own limitations could be a powerful force in my life (maybe in MANY lives), and that something so much more important than just my disability, itself, could come of it.

Adversity is a certainty in life. It might look different to every single one of us, but the underlying challenge is the same. Understanding and accepting it, getting through it, and ideally, transforming the experience.

The truth about things that suck? They suck. They're not fun and some-times, that means we're not okay for a minute or two. But it's possible to have two truths that coexist at the same time…the second truth is that there is a lot we can learn, a lot we can do and a lot of gifts that the sucky things bring to our lives and that empower us to be better and to make the world better.

Acknowledgements

There is no greater gift you can give a person than to believe in them, and I have been so fortunate to have so many exceptional people in my life who told me "I could."

Thank you to my parents for being strong role models, for encouraging my goals and for not letting me make excuses.

To Michael—my husband. For choosing the life with me every day that I have no choice but to live. Thank you for believing that I could capture every crazy dream I've had and for giving me the latitude in our partnership to pursue them.

My daughter, Grace—you gave me the greatest gift of all when I became your mom. I love you more than I ever thought it possible to love another human.

To my sister, Jennifer—thank you for being my constant friend, for your example of kindness, and for all the times you said on Facebook that you were proud of me when I was stepping into a new dream of being a speaker. When my insecurity flared and my imposter syndrome bubbled and I wondered what in the world I was even doing, your words meant a lot.

Eileen, my best friend—you changed me. I can't even find the words to articulate all you have taught me, but it had a lot to do with showing me the kind of person I wanted to be. My life would be so very different if you had not shown up when you did, and I am so utterly grateful for you.

And, to the experts—my heroes—who gave me time they didn't have in order to encourage me and to help me believe in myself:

- To Dave Hollis—who mentored me through this book process, expecting nothing in return.
- To Scott Miller. Your generous spirit is one I aspire to. Thank you for giving me time and information, for making introductions, for time on your podcast, and for being a friend.
- To Shawn Achor, who answered this stranger's random email and then granted me an interview so I could learn valuable perspective this book needed.
- To Rachel Hollis. As a stranger in the lobby of our lash-extension salon who, when I told you I was an aspiring motivational speaker, you replied, "and what are you doing to make that happen?" You made me believe I actually could. Truly—that day changed everything about what career I would pursue.
- And Mally Roncal, for being kind and strong, fun and positive and for encouraging me. For making me feel like I mattered.

Taylor Ellison and the "We Are Austin" team—thank you for embracing putting my "Morning Motivations" on television and putting a girl in a wheelchair in your viewers direct line-of-sight regularly.

To Melinda Garvey and Cy White of *Austin Woman Magazine*. Thank you for giving my writing its first professional platform and for welcoming me into your world. It has been an honor to support YOUR mission!

To Mike Blishak. You believed in me twelve years ago when I first began this journey to publish a book. You believed in me more than I did back then, and I hope that *this* book makes you proud.

Jean Cozad Poteet, thank you for being a maniacal cheerleader and for always knowing everything I need to know about everything I want to do. Also for not laughing when I say, "I have an idea."

To Shannan Hale, for always rooting for the underdog and for believing in my dreams.

For every Personal Care Assistant I have ever had on my team. You are the arms and legs I need to live this crazy life I've created. You are more important to me than I can ever tell you, and my gratitude for what you have done—and continue to do—every single day for me is deep. Thank you for being such an important part of my life.

To Natalie, Pamela, Sally and Madison for honoring me with your hard stories. Thank you for entrusting them to me and for allowing me to make them a valuable part of this book's teachings.

To my heroes who I *don't* know, but who have inspired my dreams and made me passionate about them—Barbara Mandrell, Trisha Yearwood, Garth Brooks, Marie Forleo, Gabby Bernstein, Brene Brown.

To Oprah—for being in a category of inspiration all your own.

Oh my goodness—to everyone I have ever encountered at the Muscular Dystrophy Association. What you gave me in my childhood, teen and young adult years not only supported my health journey and produced a life-saving treatment, but my partnership with you helped me see the potential for my life. Every single moment of every interaction with all of you directly influenced the trajectory of my life.

My agent, Chip MacGregor. You were the one person I needed to say, "yes." Thank you for believing in what I had to say and for helping me get it over the finish line.

Dave, Matt and Colin at Woodhall Press. For turning my life-long dream into a reality.

And to the readers – thank you for taking this journey with me. I wrote this book for you and hope you found joy and perspective and encouragement here. Look to the future and see the possibilities ahead.

About the Author

Mindy Henderson gave her first speech at the age of four as the Texas State Ambassador for the Muscular Dystrophy Association (MDA). Through her early work with MDA, Mindy found her voice and learned that she had contributions to make. She credits these early experiences with helping her to understand there is beauty and purpose to be found in adversity. Mindy has earned a Bachelor's and a Master's degree. She worked corporate jobs in high-tech for 20 years, advancing steadily up the corporate ladder. In 2005, Mindy was commissioned to write an article about her Chinese adoption of her daughter for MDA's national "Quest" magazine, and was a "Featured Blogger" on MDA's national website from 2013-2014. Mindy pivoted from her 20 year full-time work in the high-tech corporate world, to building a platform as a motivational speaker, where she shares her message and the tools she has acquired to help her overcome not only her disability, but recovery from two devastating automobile accidents and job losses and more. Mindy currently resides in Austin, Texas.